High Performance Computing
Demystified

About the Cover

Aircraft Design

Computation: Dino Roman, John Vassberg, and Tom Gruschaus, Douglas Aircraft Company. *Visualization:* Richard Charles, San Diego Supercomputer Center, using FAST (Flow Analysis Software Toolkit) on a Silicon Graphics Iris workstation.

Computer models are useful for testing aircraft design without building expensive prototypes. A computational fluid dynamics simulation of an aircraft in flight was conducted by Douglas Aircraft Company engineers and visualized at the San Diego Supercomputer Center. Tracer particles were released into the flow field in front of the aircraft and allowed to follow the streamlines around the vehicle. A cutting plane through the three-dimensional volume of data was placed to intersect the aircraft fuselage and wings. Colored contours represent the air pressure on the right side and air speed on the left.

High Performance Computing Demystified

David Loshin

AP PROFESSIONAL

Boston   San Diego   New York
London   Sydney   Tokyo   Toronto

This book is printed on acid-free paper ∞

Copyright © 1994 by Academic Press, Inc.
All rights reserved.
No part of this publication may be reproduced or
transmitted in any form or by any means, electronic
or mechanical, including photocopy, recording, or
any information storage and retrieval system, without
permission in writing from the publisher.

Portions of this material have been adapted with permission
of HPCWire, San Diego, CA.

AP PROFESSIONAL
955 Massachusetts Avenue, Cambridge, MA 02139

An imprint of ACADEMIC PRESS, INC.
A Division of HARCOURT BRACE & COMPANY

United Kingdom Edition published by
ACADEMIC PRESS LIMITED
24–28 Oval Road, London NW1 7DX

Library of Congress Cataloging-in-Publication Data
Loshin, David S.
    High performance computing demystified / David Loshin.
       p.   cm.
    Includes bibliographical references and index.
    ISBN 0-12-455825-9
    1. Electronic digital computers.   2. Computer software.
I. Title.
QA76.5.L67   1994
004'.35--dc20   94-5256
                                                            CIP

Printed in the United States of America

94 95 96 97   IP   9 8 7 6 5 4 3 2 1

Contents

Foreword		xi
Preface		xv
I	**Introduction and History**	**1**
1	**Introduction**	**3**
	1.1 Introduction	3
	1.2 What Is High Performance?	3
	1.3 Who Uses High Performance Computers?	4
	1.4 Analysis Metrics	7
	1.5 Structure	9
2	**History**	**13**
	2.1 The History of High Performance	13
	2.2 Classes of High Performance Machines	14
	2.3 Vector Processing	15
	2.4 Multiprocessor Supercomputers	17
	2.5 Advances in Microprocessor Design	20
	2.6 The Future: Putting It Together	20
II	**Computer Architectures**	**23**
3	**High Performance on a Chip**	**25**
	3.1 Killer Micros	25
	3.2 What Makes a High Performance Chip?	25
	3.3 How Processors Are Made Fast	27
	3.4 RISC Machines	29
	3.5 The Memory Bottleneck	33
	3.6 Conclusion	43

4 Topological Issues — 45
- 4.1 Connectivity — 46
- 4.2 Switches — 46
- 4.3 Topologies and Routing — 48
- 4.4 Network Functionality — 55
- 4.5 New Trends in Communications — 57

III Multiple Processor Architectures — 59

5 Vector Processors — 61
- 5.1 Pipelined Supercomputers — 61
- 5.2 Vector Instructions — 64
- 5.3 Early Pipelined Computers: Examples — 64
- 5.4 Later Pipelined Computers — 65
- 5.5 Attached Processors — 66
- 5.6 New Directions — 70

6 Multiprocessor Machines — 73
- 6.1 Parallelism — 73
- 6.2 Coordination and Synchronization — 75
- 6.3 Memory Models — 75
- 6.4 Programming Models — 82
- 6.5 Hardware Issues — 84

7 Collections of Workstations — 91
- 7.1 The Cluster Model — 91
- 7.2 Networks of Workstations — 92
- 7.3 Future Goals — 94
- 7.4 Example — 94

8 I/O — 97
- 8.1 Introduction — 97
- 8.2 RAID — 97
- 8.3 Internal Parallel I/O Systems — 98
- 8.4 External I/O Systems — 99
- 8.5 Conclusion — 103

IV Software Issues 105

9 Software 107
- 9.1 Languages 107
- 9.2 Compilers 117
- 9.3 Operating Systems 132
- 9.4 Message Passing Systems 134
- 9.5 Reliability in Distributed Systems 138

V High Performance Applications 141

10 Models of Physical Systems 143
- 10.1 Introduction 143
- 10.2 The Need for High Performance 144
- 10.3 Heat Conduction 145
- 10.4 Fluid Flow 145
- 10.5 Methods for Solving the Equations 148
- 10.6 Problem Decomposition 152
- 10.7 Other Applications 153
- 10.8 Conclusion 157

11 Seismic Applications 159
- 11.1 Introduction 159
- 11.2 The Need for High Performance 159
- 11.3 Seismic Exploration 160
- 11.4 Seismic Processing 161
- 11.5 Analysis of Geophysical Data 161
- 11.6 Reservoir Modeling 167
- 11.7 Summary 168

12 Biology and Artificial Life 169
- 12.1 Biology and High Performance Computing 169
- 12.2 Computational Biochemistry 169
- 12.3 Neural Networks 174
- 12.4 Memory-Based Reasoning 177
- 12.5 Artificial Life 179
- 12.6 Conclusion 181

13 Business Applications — **183**
- 13.1 Introduction — 183
- 13.2 Large Database Applications — 184
- 13.3 Decision Support — 184
- 13.4 Data Mining and Micromarketing — 186
- 13.5 Intelligent Business Software — 187
- 13.6 Example in Parallelization: Options Pricing — 188
- 13.7 Conclusion — 193

14 Optimization — **197**
- 14.1 Introduction — 197
- 14.2 The Need for High Performance — 197
- 14.3 Formalization — 198
- 14.4 The Simplex Method — 202
- 14.5 Airline Crew Pairing — 204
- 14.6 Portfolio Management — 206
- 14.7 Summary — 212

15 Graphics and Visualization — **213**
- 15.1 Introduction — 213
- 15.2 The Need for High Performance — 213
- 15.3 A Graphics Technique: Ray Tracing — 214
- 15.4 Parallel Graphics Processing — 218
- 15.5 Specialized Hardware: SGI's RealityEngine — 219
- 15.6 Visualization — 220
- 15.7 Virtual Reality — 221

VI Availability — **225**

16 Conclusion — **227**
- 16.1 Timely, Timeless, or What? — 227
- 16.2 National Laboratories — 227
- 16.3 Hard Copy Publications — 232
- 16.4 Online Information — 234
- 16.5 Manufacturers — 235

Glossary — **239**

Bibliography — **247**

Index — **253**

List of Figures

2.1	Shared memory	19
3.1	Instruction pipelining	31
3.2	Memory hierarchies	35
4.1	A fully connected graph with five vertices	46
4.2	A partially connected graph	47
4.3	A two-by-two switch	47
4.4	Data paths through a two-by-two switch	48
4.5	Omega network	49
4.6	Ring network	50
4.7	Order 0, 1, and 2 hypercubes	51
4.8	Order 3 and 4 hypercubes	52
4.9	A fat-tree network	54
4.10	Two-dimensional mesh	55
4.11	Three-dimensional mesh	56
5.1	Partial results propagate through the pipeline	63
5.2	SIMD computer: control processor and network of processing elements	67
5.3	The PE mesh on the ILLIAC IV	69
6.1	Shared memory multiple processor system with n processors and k memories	76
6.2	Distributed memory multiple processor system with n processors and n memories	81
6.3	Distribution of arrays across a 100-processor MPP machine	89
8.1	Disks attached to each node	100
8.2	Disks attached to network	101

List of Figures

8.3	Disks attached to dedicated I/O nodes	102
9.1	Array section assignment	110
9.2	Array assignment using `FORALL`	113
9.3	Before parallelization	127
9.4	Parallelized loops allocated to processors N and M	128
9.5	Data dependence graph for example 1	130
9.6	Data dependence graph for example 2	131
10.1	Heat conduction along a metal rod	149
10.2	Discretized view of the metal rod	150
11.1	Seismic waves are "shot" from the source and received at the receiver	162
12.1	A neurode	175
13.1	Single processor C code for options pricing	192
13.2	Data parallel HPF code for options pricing	194
14.1	A typical risk vs. return plot.	208
14.2	An example of a binomial lattice	210
15.1	Projection onto a two-dimensional surface	215

Foreword

When I was a kid, 25 years ago, I dreamed of having a computer in my basement. This was about as impossible as wishing to own a supersonic airplane, but it made for pleasant daydreams. I did have the use of an IBM 1130 at school, a small scientific computer that ran at the tremendous speed of 100,000 instructions per second (with 8,000 bytes of memory). But I wanted one all to myself.

In college and graduate school, I dreamed of having my own PDP-10. In 1975, that was a standard high-end computer for university research laboratories. It ran at 1,000,000 instructions per second, had 1,000,000 bytes of memory, and cost about $1,000,000. There was also a box about the size of a refrigerator called a "laser printer"—one of the very first ones, Even if, by a great stretch of the imagination, I could own a PDP-10, a laser printer was obviously out of the question.

In 1987, I drove to my local personal computer store and bought a Macintosh II and a laser printer. Over 1,000,000 instructions per second; 4,000,000 bytes of memory; better and faster printing from a printer the size of a breadbox; and all for half the price of a new car. (Today you can get the same for a tenth the price of a new car.) And millions of other people own the same thing or better.

Now I dream of owning a supercomputer.

In 1975, when I was using that PDP-10, the Cray-1 burst on the scene. At 100,000,000 instructions per second, it became the new standard against which all other supercomputers were measured.

But today you can buy a single-chip microprocessor that is even faster. Even more amazing, the world's faster computer today is over 1,000 times as fast as the Cray-1.

How is this possible? How can it be that computers keep getting faster and faster? The speed of the world's fastest computer doubles about every two years or so. That has been going on for forty years now, and may continue to do so for the next twenty. Doubling in speed every two years has made today's supercomputers well over a million times faster than those forty years ago.

To see just how amazing this is, imagine yourself flying in the Concorde, a supersonic airplane that is about the fastest commercial means of transportation today. If transportation were to be a million times faster, you'd have to travel faster than light. Professor Einstein advised me not to bet the farm on that one.

If you ask many persons in the computer industry how computers can keep getting faster and faster, they will speak of "process improvements" and "advancements in technology"; but to me that misses the main point. The secret is that we don't speed up computers only by speeding up a given physical process. The point of a computer is not to achieve a physical process but to process information, to computer. And —this is the key—we can change the way in which information is represented physically and still get the same informational result.

At the beginning of time (that is, in the 1940s), information might be stored as vibrations in a pool of mercury, or as electrostatic charges on a TV-like screen, or as the direction of the magnetic field in a tiny doughnut-shaped piece of magnetic ceramic. Today we use integrated circuits made of silicon, and information is stored as electrostatic charges in capacitors so tiny they can't be seen with the naked eye. And yet, all these computers, if programmed appropriately, can carry out the exact same computations on the exact same information.

Maybe we could make transportation a million times faster if we could invent something like the *Star Trek* transporter. Such a breakthrough effectively changes the rules of the game. The rules for building computers have several times thus changed; we seem to keep finding breakthroughs that allow information to be represented in ways that are more and more efficient and cost-effective. (Interestingly enough, in the original *Star Trek* series there seemed to be an assumption that the transporter actually moved physical objects. In *Star Trek: The Next Generation*, some episodes imply that a computer has gotten into the act, allowing it to screen out bacteria and weapons during the transfer; perhaps the writers intend us to understand that an object is converted to information, processed, and then reconstituted at the other end.)

The world's fastest computers can now do astonishing things. To see this, you need only visit your local movie theater and admire the computer-assisted special effects in such movies as *Terminator II*, *Jurassic Park*, and *The Lion King*. The computer doesn't make a movie camera run faster or spray paint more quickly onto animation cels; rather, the problem is converted into a mat-

Foreword

ter of information processing, the supercomputer does its amazingly fast thing, and at the very end the information is converted back to the desired physical form. This same strategy of converting a problem to informational form and back has been tremendously successful not only for entertainment but for industrial and commercial applications.

In this book, David Loshin introduces you to supercomputers: what they are made of, how they work, and—most important of all—how they are used. He does discuss "nuts and bolts," but fully half this book is devoted to supercomputer software and applications. How supercomputers are programmed and how they are put to work are most important because that is what will survive. The physical technology has changed many times and will change again. I have absolutely no idea what the supercomputers of the year 2014 will look like or what they will be made of, but I confidently predict that they will be a thousand times faster than today's supercomputers, that the information processing strategies of today will still be in use, and that, purely by virtue of their additional information processing speed, they will accomplish feats completely undreamed of today.

I rather doubt we'll ever manage to build a transporter. But I bet we have holodecks.

Boy, would I like to have one in my basement...

Guy L. Steele Jr.
Cambridge, Massachusetts

Preface

Everywhere we look these days, it is apparent that many millions of dollars are directed toward the development and sales of high performance computers. Almost every day, both the *New York Times* and the *Wall Street Journal* have articles dedicated to high performance computing. The President talks about plans for an "information data superhighway." These are intriguing issues, yet, what makes a computer a high performance computer? Who are the people who build them, and who are the people who use them?

This book is meant to be a discussion of high performance computing. It is targeted at an informed audience of engineers and business managers who have a basic understanding of computers and would like to learn about high performance computing. There are two goals in presenting this material. The first is to "demystify" high performance computing by providing an overview for non-experts of existing high performance resources. This includes describing numerous current and future applications across many disciplines. The second goal is to demonstrate that in the future, all computers will have the power or structure of today's high performance computers. By understanding the issues, the reader will be well informed regarding computing resources of the future.

The book is divided into five parts. The first part is an introduction and a history of high performance computing. The second part is a description of the "basic" parts needed to build high performance computers. This includes high performance microprocessors and network topologies. The third part includes descriptions of multiprocessor architectures of high performance: large number crunchers, massively parallel processing (MPP) machines, and networks of workstations. The fourth part describes software paradigms for high performance. The first part describes a number of applications that are well suited for high performance computers; this is shown using case studies. The final part describes the high performance computing resources that are available to the public, with some guide to accessing those resources.

Thanks go first to the people at AP PROFESSIONAL, whose help has guided me from the beginning of this project: Chuck Glaser, Cindy Kogut, Karen Pratt, and Mary Treseler.

The following people helped with reviewing, and their assistance helped guide the early development of this project: John Pates, Lou Zand, Tom Tabor, Mitch Loebel, Norris Parker Smith, and David Loveman.

I would like to thank the members of the Programming Environments group at Thinking Machines, and in particular Robert Millstein, Stan Vestal, and Phil Lynch.

I would like to note the help of the following people, who were kind enough to spend time reviewing the many technical issues covered in this book: Skef Wholey, Mark Buxbaum, Gary Sabot, Cliff Lasser, John Ruttenberg, David Presburg, Zdenek Johan, Leo Unger, Robert Ferrell, David Lively, David Gingold, Rob Jones, Doug Newell, Stephen Smith, Ralph Mor, Karl Sims, Peter Loshin, Marshall Isman, Ken Birman, Al Geist, and Sandy Raymond.

I would especially like to thank the following people, who were kind enough to spend many hours discussing the topics covered in this book: Guy Steele, Woody Lichtenstein, Richard Shapiro, Bruce Boghosian, Jonathan Eckstein, Mark Dobson, Denny Dahl, and Larry Morley.

David Loshin
Cambridge, Massachusetts

About the Cover

The cover illustration is a computer-generated image of a cutting plane through the three-dimensional volume of an airplane. The colored image is a visualization of a computer model useful for testing aircraft design. The visualized computation was performed by Dino Roman, John Vassberg, and Tom Gruschaus of Douglas Aircraft Company, and the visualization was performed by Richard Charles of the San Diego Supercomputer Center using the Flow Analysis Software Toolkit.

Part I
Introduction and History

Chapter 1

Introduction

1.1 Introduction

Twenty years ago, the notion of a high performance machine conjured up images of an expensive monolith, with a high tech cooling system to keep the machine from overheating. Early supercomputers, crunching away at numbers in their special environments, were awe inspiring when compared to the standard mainframe computer.

The idea that the same degree of computer power could be shrunk in size down to a microprocessor chip and inserted into a desktop workstation was inconceivable. Yet, today microprocessors are available whose computing power rivals, even exceeds, the power of the CRAY-1. The computational power that can be purchased today can solve large problems in a fraction of the time of that of the supercomputers of the previous decade.

With the resources available for "desktop supercomputing," it is important to learn how to harness this computational power and understand how to make the best use of these resources. This book is meant to give an overview of high performance computing that gives a good level of understanding without the frightening details.

1.2 What Is High Performance?

It is difficult to pin down a quantified definition of *high performance*. Because all computer manufacturers are constantly improving their products, striving for faster computational speed and network communication speed and bandwidth, the line between a "high performance" machine and a "regular" computer is difficult to draw. A computer considered to be a supercomputer twenty years ago is slow compared to some of today's desktop machines.

But certain characteristics can be used to differentiate high performance machines from their non-supercomputer counterparts. High performance machines typically are characterized by high speed computation, a large main memory, and a large secondary memory system. High performance often means faster overall speed of computation. This is most often achieved in one of two ways: making sequential computation faster, computing in parallel, or at the high end, both.

A good way to talk about high performance is to talk about the kinds of problems that require significant computing power to solve. These problems usually require a lot of computations and operate over large data sets. Traditionally, members of the scientific community have been the definers of the problems needing supercomputers; they have referred to these as *grand challenge* problems. These grand challenge problems are the focal point of the push for faster, more efficient machines known as the teraflops race.

Another aspect of high performance is the use of high speed input and output systems for flowing data in and out of the processing units as quickly as possible. Also, high speed data interconnects can be used to attach low-end machines to form a "virtual supercomputer."

Many of the scientific problems have related applications in industry, and so the benefits of using a high performance system are transferred into the business community. Also, the availability of high speed systems has inspired members of the business community to adapt their projects to take advantage of high performance machines.

1.3 Who Uses High Performance Computers?

High performance computer users can be characterized at a high level as those who purchase computer systems and services to solve real and abstract problems by computer modeling, simulation, and analysis, perform Computer Aided Design, or create software and systems solutions for sale to aid these users.

The truth is that high performance computers are becoming more mainstream as the technology curve brings megaflops to the desktop. In particular, though, traditional users of high performance machines have fallen into these categories, among others:

1.3. Who Uses High Performance Computers?

- *High Energy Physics.* Many physical problems require large numbers of computing cycles. Imagine trying to model the interaction between all the subatomic particles released at the time of the Big Bang. A field of study in high energy physics, quantum chromodynamics (or more commonly, QCD), examines the interaction between different kinds of quarks and other subatomic particles. Not only has QCD been an important application programmed for high performance computers, a specific multiple processor machine was constructed at Columbia University specifically to compute solutions to the QCD problem!

- *Semiconductor Industry, VLSI Design.* Chip designers attempting to lay out a design on a silicon chip encounter issues dealing with the crossing of wires, heating, and overlays. When trying to place over 3 million transistors on a wafer smaller than your fingernail, chip designers use programs that will compile a description of a chip into a viable layout. These programs are compute–intensive, and a high performance machine is suitable for this problem.

- *Graphics and Virtual Reality.* Computer animation with fine detail needs significant computing power. Generating computer graphics is a very computation-intensive process. High performance machines have been used for automatic mapping of textures to surfaces, for creating new graphic images, and for virtual reality. A good example of virtual graphic images integrated into "real life" is the way that computer-generated dinosaurs chase characters in the movie *Jurassic Park*.

- *Weather and Ocean Modeling.* Predicting the weather, as well as modeling the movement of ocean currents are two applications that are well suited to high performance computers. Being able to predict weather patterns such as hurricanes or tornados enough in advance to save lives is difficult unless a supercomputer is used.

- *Visualization.* Given a database full of information, users will want to see a representation of their data without having to read thousands of individual records. Through visualization programs, the data can be manipulated into a form that is easily understandable, such as a three-dimensional graph.

- *Oil Industry.* The oil industry has different uses for high performance computing. One example is analysis of seismic data. Before an oil company will invest large amounts of money in drilling for oil, that company will collect information about the area that is to be drilled. That data is then analyzed using high performance computers to determine where the best place to drill is.

Another example is reservoir simulation. This involves modeling the flow of oil and other liquids through porous material.

- *Automobile Industry.* Automobile designers like to model the flow of air around the chassis of a car. But building a real model, then performing the actual tests can be avoided if computer models will accurately display the flow of air. In essence, the computer is being used as a "numerical wind tunnel."

  Also, crash analysis, a very important application, is expensive when using real versions of the automobile. By using computer simulation, crashes may be modeled and analyzed at a much lower cost. High performance machines are needed to create and analyze these models in real time.

- *Chemicals and Pharmaceuticals Industry.* Pharmaceutical manufacturers are constantly trying to create new drugs. Programs exist that can be used to model new molecular structures and to predict their behaviors under certain situations.

- *Financial Applications.* High performance computers are used to help portfolio managers build successful hedged portfolios.

- *Business Applications.* Large databases that are unmanageable by workstation standards are easily digested by high performance computers. Credit card companies may use high performance computers to predict when card holders are about to cancel their cards. Mail order companies may use supercomputers to determine which customers are more likely to buy certain kinds of items. The porting of database application systems such as Oracle and SQL to supercomputers allows companies to "mine information" out of their huge databases.

- *Airline Industry.* Optimization problems such as optimal scheduling of airline crews or matching airplanes to scheduled routes are more easily solved using high power computational systems.

1.4 Analysis Metrics

We can define certain metrics that can be used to analyze high performance. Typically, a high performance system will help solve large problems in a reasonable amount of time. To a high energy physicist, a reasonable amount of time may be one year. To a Wall Street options pricer, one hour may not be reasonable. Ultimately, a user must gauge the performance level of a computer system by the time it takes for the user's specific problems to be solved.

We can use different measurement techniques to determine whether a computer is a high performance machine. Many of these techniques are useful in some ways but misleading in other ways. A list of metrics that can be used to characterize high performance follows.

Peak Performance

The **peak performance** of a machine is the absolute top speed that the machine can operate. This is the upper limit on the speed of a processor imposed by the physical structure of the machine. Saying that a computer has a peak performance of 100 GFLOPS means that the fastest *any* process can run on that computer is 100 GFLOPS.

The peak performance is a theoretical limit, based on the hardware constraints of the central processing unit (**CPU**). Most programs that run on a computer are not specifically bound to pure CPU execution; a certain amount of interaction with the outside is necessary. This interaction includes collecting operands from the memory system or waiting for I/O. Because most, if not all programs must perform some extra-CPU interactions, it is rare that any applications run at the sustained peak performance of any machine.

Sustained Performance

Sustained performance is the highest consistently achieved speed of a machine. Sustained performance is a good way of describing the general performance of a machine, since it represents a level of performance that can be attained on a regular basis. Instead of using the peak performance, talking about the sustained performance gives a more realistic view of what a user may expect out of a high performance machine.

As the peak performance of a machine increases, in general so does the sustained performance, but the percent of peak performance represented by the sustained performance decreases. For example, doubling the clock speed of a machine will increase the peak performance by 2, but the sustained performance will increase by less than 2 due to memory access limitations.

Cost/Performance

The cost/performance of a machine is a figure of the amount of performance per dollar spent for that machine, based on a chosen performance metric. This metric is often used to compare different kinds of high performance hardware. For example, suppose a machine that attains a sustained 10 GFLOPS costs $10 million and a machine that attains a sustained 100 MFLOPS costs $50,000. The cost/performance ratio (or C/P ratio) for the 10 GFLOPS machine is

$$\frac{\$10,000,000}{10 \times 10^9 \text{ FLOPS}}$$

or $1000 for each MFLOPS.

The C/P ratio for the 100 MFLOPS machine is

$$\frac{\$50,000}{100 \times 10^6 \text{ FLOPS}}$$

or $500 for each FLOPS.

Note that using the cost/performance metric, the smaller machine is more cost effective. In general, very fast machines are not the most cost effective; often cost-effectiveness is sacrificed for higher performance.

Speedup

Speedup is a term used to describe the proportional difference in running time of an algorithm executed on multiple processors compared to the running time of the same algorithm on a single processor. Formally, the speedup attained on a problem of size N using P processors is calculated as

$$S_P(N) = \frac{T_1(N)}{T_P(N)}.$$

1.5. Structure

Measuring speedup can give the applications programmer an idea about the degree of parallelism achieved using a specific algorithm.

1.5 Structure

This book is meant to be an introduction to the world of high performance computing. Despite having just presented some performance metrics, this book is not designed to be a supercomputer buyer's guide, but rather a simplified illumination of some of the more important issues in the high performance arena. Specific machines will not be compared with respect to those analysis metrics except when useful in explaining a more important point. Ideally, a reader who completes this book will be prepared to take on some of the more challenging texts listed in the bibliography. The text is broken up into these parts.

- **Introduction and History:** This part provides an introduction, followed by a discussion of the evolution of supercomputers and high performance machines.

- **Basic Hardware Issues:** This part discusses some basic hardware objects. There is a chapter on high performance using microprocessors, a chapter on topological issues, and a chapter on I/O issues.

- **Advanced Hardware Configurations:** This part builds on what was discussed in the previous part by discussing more complex high performance systems. There is a chapter on vector processing, a chapter on multiple processor systems, and a chapter that discusses collections of workstations.

- **Software Issues:** This part consist of a chapter that covers some important issues regarding software development for high performance systems. The chapter talks about high performance programming languages, message passing schemes, and some operating systems issues.

- **Solution Methods and Applications:** We will look at some of the details of certain kinds of applications, and why those applications are suited to high performance computers. Each of these chapters is meant to be an introduction to a set of applications. Although the world of high performance applications is much larger than the set of applications we discuss, this particular set is meant as a general introduction.

Many physical model applications fall into the category of differential equation applications. Fluid mechanics, structural mechanics, and heat conduction are examples of systems governed by the laws of physics. These laws are stated in the form of differential equations. This chapter will discuss two methods used for solving differential equations using high performance computers: the finite element method and the finite difference method.

Because the need for supercomputer capability in the oil industry is great, we will have a chapter that discusses two applications pertinent to the petroleum business: exploration and reservoir modeling.

A number of applications related to biology will be covered in this chapter, including the modeling of protein folding, custom-made pharmaceutical drugs, and the use of high performance computing in CAT scans and MRI scans. This chapter will also discuss artificial life applications, such as cellular automata and neural networks.

Problems of finding an optimal solution to a large problem, such as the airline problems and the portfolio management problems mentioned earlier will be discussed in this chapter.

Large database management systems, as well as artificial intelligent programs for prediction in business will be discussed in this chapter. In addition, we will see how a simple financial derivative pricing program can be implemented on a high performance machine.

Finally, we will look at some of the issues regarding graphics applications, as well as look at topics of virtual reality in this chapter.

- **How to Find out More and Conclusion:** The national supercomputer centers will be discussed. Also, there is a directory of high performance computer manufacturers and how to get more information, along with a listing of other sources of information on high performance computing.

- **Glossary:** A glossary of terms used in the world of high performance computing closes the text.

Certain discussions require programming examples. These examples will be expressed using `this typeface`.

1.5. Structure

> **Sidebars**
>
> Interesting information that relates to the subject being discussed will appear in sidebars such as this.

> Useful definitions will appear in doubly enclosed boxes such as this.

If you use a computer, eventually you will be using a high performance machine, for as the technology for building high performance machines advances, and the development of software that straddles the boundary between desktop and supercomputers continues, eventually the power of the most expensive high performance machines will be available at the desktop.

Chapter 2

History

2.1 The History of High Performance

The development of high performance machines has advanced over the past 30 years. While advances in processor design have allowed hardware makers to reduce the time of computation, thereby increasing scalar computation speed, greater advances in high performance computing can be attributed to hardware designed for parallel computation. Parallel supercomputer architecture had traditionally been broken up into three distinct kinds:[1]

- Pipelined supercomputers

- Vector supercomputers

- Multiprocessor supercomputers

In addition, high speed memory systems have been developed to keep up with the processor performance. The different kinds of memories are connected into hierarchical levels, where memory that is accessible quickly is closely connected to the computation hardware and the slower access memory is located at a farther distance. The different kinds of memories include cache memories, secondary caches, high speed primary memory banks, lower level primary memory banks, and fast secondary memory systems (such as high speed disks). The way that these memory levels are interconnected (referred to as the *memory hierarchy*), is also related to high performance

---

[1] Hwang, *Supercomputers: Design and Applications*, pg. 5

computation. This includes interleaved memory buses to increase memory bandwidth, and redundant disk arrays for parallel storage.

Over time, the development of high performance machines using these techniques allowed the evolution of computers that use combinations of these technologies. Looking at the history of design of high performance computers, it is evident that the development philosophy has come full circle, and techniques used 20 years ago for the largest supercomputers are employed today to build high performance microprocessors!

2.2 Classes of High Performance Machines

Parallel processor machines allow for different kinds of **parallelism**. When distinct processors execute different paths of a computation, that is called *control parallelism*. When distinct processors execute the same program on different bits of data, that is referred to as *data parallelism*. If an application is broken up into different executable pieces and each piece is allocated to a specific processor in a multiprocessor environment, that is referred to as *task parallelism*.

Traditionally, supercomputers have been grouped into categories of architectures that reflect the relationship between the hardware and the kind of parallelism:

- *SISD.* SISD is an acronym for single instruction stream, single data stream. Conventional sequential computers fall into this category, where a single processing unit executes a sequential stream of operations on a single stream of data.

- *SIMD.* SIMD is an acronym for single instruction stream, multiple data stream. Array processor machines fall into this category, where a collection of processors execute the identical sequence of instructions on different data streams.

- *MISD.* MISD is an acronym for multiple instruction stream, single data stream. In this category of machines a collection of processors execute different instruction streams on one data stream.

- *MIMD.* MIMD is an acronym for multiple instruction stream, multiple data stream. Multiple processor machines may belong to this category, where a collection of processors execute different instruction sequences on different data streams.

2.3 Vector Processing

The development of vector processors is more easily understood when accompanied by an explanation of the vector programming model. In simple terms, **vector processing** means executing the same arithmetic operation over a grouped collection of operands. For example, consider this Fortran example:

```
REAL A(128), B(128), C(128), X
   .
   .
   .
DO I = 1, 128, 1
   A(I) = X*B(I) + C(I)
ENDDO
   .
   .
   .
```

This is a Fortran DO loop, in which each of the 128 elements of the array B is multiplied by the variable X, added to the corresponding element of the array C and then stored to the corresponding element of the array A. In a scalar processor, these operations are performed sequentially; i.e., the operations are performed over element 1 of the arrays, then over element 2, etc. In a vector computer, one operation may be performed over a vector of elements at the same time. For example, in a vector machine with a vector length of 128, the DO loop could be performed in one sequence of steps:

1. Load 128 elements of array B
2. Load X
3. Load 128 elements of array C
4. Multiply elements of array B by X
5. Add the elements of array C
6. Store the 128 elements into array A

In a vector-style programming language, such as High Performance Fortran, this loop could be written in an explicit vector form:

```
    A(1:128) = X*B(1:128) + C(1:128)
```

In a vector processor machine, parallelism is achieved through executing vector operations. In the preceding example, the entire loop executes in the same time it takes for a single iteration to execute on a serial machine. Of course, no machine has an infinite vector length. Often, the vector length is set to a specific value, such as 8 or 16. In these cases, arbitrarily lengthened loops must be broken down into a sequence of operations over subvectors of length equal to the machine's vector length. Using the preceding programming example and assuming a computer with vector length 8, the 128 element array would be operated on in chunks of 8 elements, yielding a loop of this form:

```
DO SL = 1, 128, 8
   A(SL:SL+7) = X*B(SL:SL+7) + C(SL:SL+7)
ENDDO
```

That is, loop from 1 to 128 in chunks of 8, and perform the requisite arithmetic operations over vectors of size 8.

Vector Processing: History

The early supercomputers were designed to perform well on large scale vector and matrix computations that are common to scientific programs. Vector processing was available in systems that were configured as vector supercomputers, such as Control Data Corporation's Star-100 and the TI-ASC (Advanced Scientific Computer) from Texas Instruments. These machines had the capacity for vector operations.

Later vector supercomputers had instruction sets that contained relatively sophisticated vector instructions. Instructions for arithmetic operations (ADD, SUBTRACT, MULTIPLY) as well as more complex matrix operations (DOT-PRODUCT, MERGE) were supplied. These machines, such as the CYBER 205, the CRAY-1, and the Fujitsu VP-200, became available in the middle 1970s.

Another group of vector instructions available on these machines were indirect memory instructions, such as GATHER and SCATTER. Scientific programs often employ indirect addressing operations, as do sorting and reordering algorithms. The GATHER operation, which collects data through an indirection array, can be programmed in Fortran 77,

```
INTEGER I, N
REAL A(128), B(128)
INTEGER IA(128)
    .
    .
    .
DO I = 1, N
   A(I) = B(IA(I))
ENDDO
```

or in array syntax,

```
INTEGER I, N
REAL A(128), B(128)
INTEGER IA(128)

A = B(IA)
```

Vector processing was also available in computer systems with attached array processors. An attached array processor is configured as a back-end computational module attached to a front-end host. The attached processor supplements the arithmetic floating point computational power of the front-end machine while the front-end can stream data in and out of the back-end through a high speed interface. Array processors allow for the loading and storing of, and operating on, operands as arrays. An early example of this is the AP-120B from Floating Point Systems. One way array processing is performed is through the use of multiple functional units to achieve a degree of vector parallelism. Another way to implement vector operations is through the use of a pipeline architecture. Some specifics of these architectures such as machines like the Burroughs Scientific Processor (BSP) and the ILLIAC–IV, will be discussed in Chapter 6.

2.4 Multiprocessor Supercomputers

An aim of high performance computer design is to improve reliability and throughput. Reliability can be improved if a number of processors perform redundant computation; if one of the processors fails, another in the system can take over the computation from the point of failure. While the topic of multiprocessor reliable systems is interesting, it is beyond the scope of this book.

If a certain amount of work can be performed by one processor, combining more than one processor into a computer may increase performance with relation to the number of processors, although the increase may not be directly proportional. This idea leads to the development of multiprocessor high performance computers. The idea of multiple processor computers evolved from the processor arrays. Processor arrays contain groups of processors, each with a certain capability. Once the restriction of SIMD computation is lifted, each individual processor may compute different operations on its own data. There is still a need for synchronization, but not to the extent needed in a vector processor.

Multiprocessor systems usually have at least two processors that are controlled by a single operating system. The methods for interaction between the processors and for sharing system resources are embedded in the operating system. A *tightly coupled* multiprocessor system allows for very fast communication between processors, while a *loosely coupled* system has a slower communication system. Processors in a tightly coupled system often work in closer synchrony than the processors in a loosely coupled system.

> Shared memory multiprocessor machines make use of shared variables. A **shared variable** is a data object that can be examined and modified by more than one process in a multiple process environment.

Because the processing units in a multiprocessor system are independent, a level of parallelism higher than pipelined operations can be achieved. On MIMD machines, scheduling different tasks to be allocated to the different processors will allow independent tasks to be completed in less time than if the tasks were scheduled sequentially on a uniprocessor system.

> Ensuring that when one process is using a shared variable, all other processes are excluded from doing the same thing is called **mutual exclusion**. If a certain computation depends on the completion of a previous computation, a system must guarantee that those two operations occur in the correct order. In general, forcing an order between any set of events is called *synchronization*. Synchronization primitives may be used to ensure mutual exclusion.

2.4. Multiprocessor Supercomputers

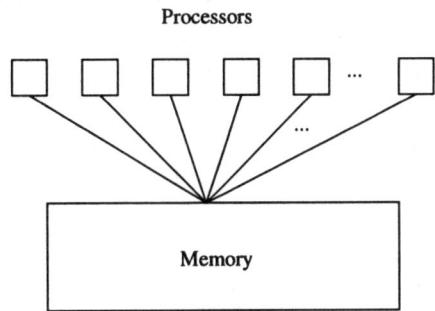

Figure 2.1: Shared memory

A traditional problem in building efficient multiprocessor systems has been controlling the bottleneck of communication and synchronization between the different processors in the system. The performance of the connecting networks could not keep up with the speed of the processors as the number of processors increased. In addition, bus architectures often did not allow for large numbers of processors to be hooked up together. Because of this, early multiprocessor computers usually did not have more than 32 processors. A different way of thinking breaks this bottleneck through the tight coupling of processors as well as computation. On SIMD machines, a large, independent computation over a large data set may be computed in tight synchrony on many processors.

Multiple processor systems have been configured as **shared-memory** systems, where all areas of memory are accessible by any of the processors. In a shared-memory system (see Figure 2.1), data are shared explicitly, and multiple accesses to shared data items must be done in a way as to maintain consistency in view among the processors. This implies the need for both synchronization and mutual exclusion primitives to protect shared data. There have also been **distributed memory** multiprocessor systems, where each processor controls its own data space, and information is shared only through explicit messages.

Cray began using more than one processor in a system in its CRAY–XMP, with two processors. Denelcor built the HEP, or Heterogeneous Element Processor, comprising 16 processors in a packet-switched network. An interesting multiple processor system was developed at the Carnegie Mellon

University. This machine, called the Cm*, consisted of clusters of processors (by LSI) connected in a hierarchical bus. The Cosmic Cube, developed at the California Institute of Technology, is a hypercube connected collection of processors. The hypercube network was later used by other multiprocessor machine manufacturers. Different kinds of multiple processor machines are discussed in Chapters 6, 7, and 8.

2.5 Advances in Microprocessor Design

Advances in Very Large Scale Integration (VLSI) technology and experience developing pipelined architectures on larger systems have enabled the implementation of high performance computing on a small scale. The ability to embed millions of transistors on a single small wafer allows powerful microprocessors to be built. The manifestation is in the widespread availability of high performance microprocessors that can be integrated into desktop systems as powerful as the CRAY-1.

2.6 The Future: Putting It Together

The direction for building high performance computers is to glean the best features of the machines just described and combine them into integrated systems. For example, the pipelining ability of early supercomputers is now standard for microprocessor design. It is interesting to note that programmers learning how to program new pipelined and multiple instruction issue processors looked to the (20 year old) literature on microcoding the early CRAY systems!

Many machines are now designed as multiprocessor systems consisting of powerful pipelined microprocessors connected in high speed networks. One example is the Connection Machine, built by Thinking Machines Corporation. The CM-5 consists of a high speed network that connects many SPARC processors. Other examples include Intel's Paragon, connecting i860 processors, and Cray's T3D, consisting of a network of Digital's Alpha chips.

What is in store for the next generations of high performance machines? Hybridization and heterogeneity could be the key words for high performance computer design of the future. Standardization of communications protocols and the stabilization of multicomputer design points to a future high performance system that consists of different kinds of computers connected with high speed links. Computation may execute across different platforms

2.6. The Future: Putting It Together

and may migrate from one system to another dynamically, in a way that is transparent to the user. The construction of the national information superhighway is a step in this direction, and should pave the way for the next generation of high performance computing.

One of the most exciting multiple processor paradigm proposals is the network of workstations. This paradigm, which has also been referred to as the workstation farm, consists of high performance workstations connected through a high speed local network. The promise of this type of system may bring the power of massive parallelism down to the desktop. This system will be discussed at greater length in a later chapter.

Part II

Computer Architectures

This part consists of two chapters. The first chapter discusses microprocessor architectures and the second, topological issues regarding networking schemes.

These chapters should be useful in reading later chapters that cover the way high performance systems integrate different kinds of processing units, using different network schemes, into multiple processor systems.

Chapter 3

High Performance on a Chip

3.1 Killer Micros

They have been called the *killer micros*. They are the high performance microprocessors that have emerged as the basis for both workstations and as nodes on multiprocessor machines. Because of their proliferation, it is thought that the high performance microprocessor may "squeeze out" the mainframe as the preeminent computational resource used in the future. The developments in VLSI design and in silicon fabrication techniques have produced microprocessors whose peak performances exceed that of the early supercomputers like the CRAY-1. This level of Cost/Performance allows high performance computing to be available to most users.

3.2 What Makes a High Performance Chip?

Electronic circuits operate and compute as a sequence of operations that occur when electrons propagate along wires in the machine. Computation "happens" when combinations of these streams of electrons meet at junctions that represent logical conditions (OR, AND, NOT). The flow of electrons is enabled when a current is applied to an enabling wire in to the computer, and the current, representing the 1 value, is applied for the length of time it takes for an electrostatic field to travel the farthest distance in that machine in one computation step. After this time has elapsed, the enabling current is turned off, and the machine is allowed to reach a steady state. This enabling current is continually cycled up and down, allowing computation to take place, and the time quantum allowed for turning the voltage up and down is called a cycle. The speed of a processor is measured in cycles per second, or Hertz (Hz); actually, a more convenient unit is millions of cycles per second, or MegaHertz (MHz). A chip said to run at a speed of 300 MHz cycles its enabling voltage line 300 million times each second. The time for the current to force the electronic field through the system, also referred to as the **clock speed**, is the generic measurement of speed for processors.

Instructions

A machine instruction is a request to the CPU to perform some computation over a set of operands (either registers or immediate values) and deposit the result in either a register or back in memory. The machine instruction is the finest grain level of computation available to the programmer. In traditional (CISC) computers, though, instructions are implemented as a composition of subcomponent operations that are delineated in *microcode*. Each instruction is executed as a sequence of microcode instructions, and because of this, each instruction may take a (different) number of cycles to complete. In fact, in some machines certain instructions, such as the divide instruction, take so many cycles to finish that programmers often encode the same operation using a sequence of instructions whose execution time totals *less* than the single long instruction!

A processor's speed is often rated as a function of the number of instructions that can be executed in a second. This measure, millions of instructions per second, or **MIPS**, is often used to compare the speed of processors.

Types of Operations

The collection of instructions for a specific processor is referred to as its instruction set. The operations that can be performed by instructions in an instruction set can be classified into four categories.

1. *Memory Operations.* These are operations that bring data in from memory and back out to memory.

2. *Integer Computations.* These are instructions that perform integer arithmetic, such as integer addition and subtraction. Logical operations such as logical AND and OR are also included in this type.

3.3. How Processors Are Made Fast

3. *Floating Point Computations.* These are operations over floating point numbers, such as floating point addition and multiplication.

4. *Branch Instructions.* These are instructions that change the flow of control in a program, such as branch instructions, the CALL instruction, and the RETURN instruction.

In CISC machines, some of the operations are combined together into single instructions. For example, an instruction that loads two values from memory, adds them, then stores the result to another memory location is not uncommon in CISC instruction sets.

Because the time to perform the floating point operations was the overwhelming factor in the time to execute a program on traditional CISC machines, another metric was developed to measure and compare machines based on their capacity for performing floating point calculations. This measurement of floating point operations per second, or **FLOPS**, is a standard ruler by which the computational powers of computers are compared.

3.3 How Processors Are Made Fast

How can the performance of a processor be increased? Using the two measurements just described, we see that the higher the MIPS or FLOPS count, the more the processor can perform in a second. Therefore, let's look at ways to increase the MIPS or FLOPS counts.

Increasing the MIPS

It is simple to determine the MIPS count of a processor if each instruction takes the same number of cycles. Unfortunately, many processor instruction sets contain instructions that take different numbers of cycles. For simplicity, let's assume an average count of 8 cycles per instruction. If the processor's clock runs at 16MHz (16 million cycles/second), and each instruction takes an average of 8 cycles, the (average) MIPS count is

$$\frac{16{,}000{,}000 \text{ cycles/second}}{8 \text{ cycles/instruction}} = 2{,}000{,}000 \text{ instructions/second}$$

or 2 MIPS.

In general, the equation for determining the MIPS of a processor whose clock speed is X MHz, when the average number of cycles per instruction is Y is

$$\frac{X \times 1{,}000{,}000 \text{ cycles/second}}{Y \text{ cycles/instruction}}$$

So, to build a processor with a higher MIPS count, the manufacturer must maximize the number of instructions executed per second. This number can be maximized in one of two ways:

1. *Increase the Clock Speed.* Increasing the clock speed will increase the dividend. When keeping the divisor (i.e., the number of cycles per instruction) constant, increasing the dividend will result in a higher value.

   The clock speed can be increased by engineering the chip such that the latency for values to propagate all the way through the processor is reduced. This is done by minimizing the length of the wires over which a current is meant to flow across the processor. Current technology allows chips with multiple layers of silicon to be fabricated; microprocessors with more than 3 million transistors are readily available.

2. *Decrease the Number of Cycles per Instruction.* If maintaining the dividend (i.e., the clock speed) constant, the result can be maximized by decreasing the divisor (i.e., the number of cycles per instruction).

   The number of cycles per instruction can be decreased in a few ways. One is to microcode the instructions more efficiently. Another way is to *pipeline* the execution of the instructions. A third way is to increase the number of functional units executing instructions. These will be discussed in detail later.

Increasing the FLOPS

To measure the FLOPS count, we compare the ratio of floating point operations that can be performed per second. Given a processor whose clock speed is X, if the fastest floating point operation takes Y cycles to complete, we can compute the FLOPS count as

$$\frac{X \times 1{,}000{,}000 \text{ cycles /second}}{Y \text{ cycles /floating point result}}$$

The way to increase the FLOPS count are similar to increasing the MIPS:

- increase the clock speed, or

- decrease the number of cycles for floating point operations.

Of course, using all of these methods to maximize the MIPS and FLOPS counts will result in a more efficient way to "speed up" a processor. This is the philosophy behind RISC and superscalar processors.

3.4 RISC Machines

Many of the high performance microprocessors are based on RISC technology. *RISC*, which stands for Reduced Instruction Set Computer, is a technology based on simplification of the operation of a microprocessor. Studies have shown that processors spend most of their time executing instructions from a limited subset of the instruction set. Moreover, the instructions in this subset are the simplest instructions. Making sure that these instructions are efficient will increase the overall efficiency of the processor. This implies building a processor with a limited set of efficient instructions.

In a RISC processor, the instruction set is limited to a small number of *necessary* instructions. Unlike CISC instructions, there is usually no combination of operations. To load two values from memory, add them and store the result back to memory, (which, as discussed before, can often be done in one CISC instruction) the RISC processor must execute four instructions: two *load*s, one *add*, and one *store*.

Making the instructions simpler has a twofold benefit:

1. The instructions can execute faster. If the instructions are simple, less overhead is needed to execute one instruction. Often, if the instructions are simple enough, there is no need for embedded microcode; the complete operation of the instruction can be described directly in hardware. In cases like this, the operation can complete in as little as one or two cycles!

2. The instructions can be implemented in a simpler way. Having a small set of simple instructions means a reduction in the amount of silicon dedicated to implementing the operations. Using less silicon to implement the instructions' logic will "free up" space for other items, such as caches and memory, to be placed on the processor wafer.

Instruction Pipelining

Instructions on a processor typically execute in four stages:

1. **FETCH.** Instructions sit in main memory, and a special register, the program counter, or **pc**, holds the address of the next instruction in memory. During the FETCH stage, the instruction itself is fetched from the location pointed to by the pc.

2. **DECODE.** Once the instruction has been loaded into the CPU, the operands must be determined and the CPU must be prepared to execute the requested operation. This is done during the DECODE stage.

3. **EXECUTE.** During the EXECUTE stage, the operation is actually performed.

4. **STORE.** The result of the operation is written to its destination (either to a register or to memory) during the STORE stage.

As soon as the FETCH phase of one instruction finishes, the processor can begin the FETCH stage of the next instruction. Similarly, as soon as the DECODE stage of one instruction has completed, the processor can begin the DECODE stage of the next instruction. The same can be said of the EXECUTE and STORE stages. When this process is repeated over a sequence of instructions, the CPU can essentially be executing parts of four instructions at the same time. This is a process called instruction pipelining (see Figure 3.1). As long as the sequence of executed instructions is long enough, the processor effectively executes an average of an instruction per clock cycle. Even though each instruction takes four cycles to execute, as long as the pipeline is full, the effective rate is one instruction cycle per clock.

Instruction pipelining is a good way to decrease the ratio of cycles per instruction. RISC processors with a single functional unit will execute an instruction every cycle. The only exception to this is when the processor

3.4. RISC Machines

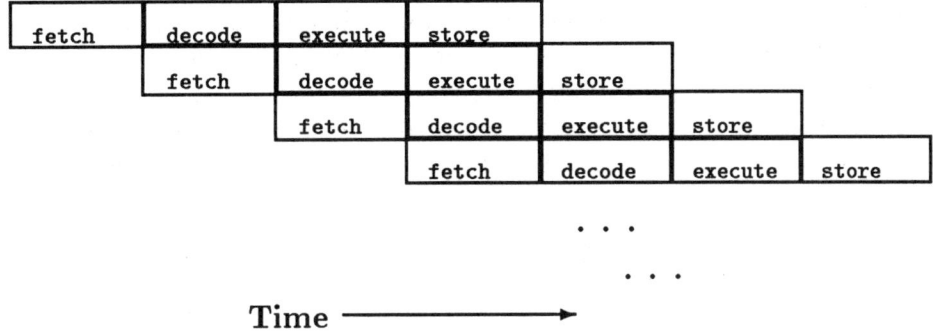

Figure 3.1: Instruction pipelining

encounters a branch instruction, since the processor has already FETCHed and DECODEd a few instructions past the branch instruction. If the branch is taken, the processor must *flush* those instructions and start up the instruction pipeline from the branched location. In this case, the instructions that followed the branch that had already been fetched and decoded are not needed, and the work to fetch and decode them is wasted. Because of this, many RISC instruction sets specify that a single instruction must be placed **after** a branch instruction! This way, at least partial benefit of the instruction pipelining is achieved: the instruction following the branch is fetched, decoded, and executed. Note, though, that any side effects the execution of that *branch slot* instruction do not affect the execution of the branch.

Multiple Instruction Issue

With instruction pipelining, a processor designer can build a chip that effectively executes an instruction on each clock cycle. To decrease the ratio of cycles per instruction even more, a processor designer must arrange for more than one instruction to be executed on each clock cycle. Since the clock cycle is the lower limit for "things to happen," the only way to get more instructions executed on each clock cycle is to have more than one processing unit on the chip.

Many RISC processors have only two functional units: an integer unit and a floating point unit. This is similar to having a floating point accelerator chip embedded inside the processor. When a processor has just one integer unit and one floating point unit, there is (usually) no reason that both units can't operate at the same time. Therefore, the instruction set provides a mechanism for initiating an integer instruction and a floating point instruction at the same time. This is called **multiple instruction issue**, and a processor that allows multiple instruction issue is said to be a **superscalar** processor.

A processor is not limited to one integer and one floating point unit. A processor can be configured with multiple integer and floating point units. Since floating point operations usually take longer than integer operations, the chip designer may achieve a greater benefit by adding multiple floating point units. In addition, a chip may have a special unit dedicated to memory instructions and perhaps another dedicated to branching instructions. To take advantage of a multiple instruction issue machine, the code that is executed must be *scheduled* is a way such that the operands used by each unit do not interfere with each other. That is, if the result of an instruction A executed by one floating point unit is used as an operand by an instruction B executed by a different floating point unit, A must complete before instruction B begins. Some RISC chips provide automatic **scoreboarding** that will stall the execution until the needed operation has completed. Other chips don't provide the scoreboarding, and therefore the programmer must schedule his or her instructions. This service is usually provided by the compiler, so the programmer does not have to worry about explicit instruction scheduling.

The addition of multiple functional units allows the processor to execute more than one instruction per cycle. This lowers the ratio of cycles per instruction so that the MIPS and FLOPS counts become greater.

Let's look at an example. Assume we have a RISC processor with two integer functional units, one floating point addition unit, and one floating point multiplication unit. The clock speed is 100 MHz. The processor can begin the execution of two integer and two floating point instructions on each cycle. This is four instructions per cycle, yielding

$$\frac{100 \times 1{,}000{,}000 \text{ cycles/second}}{\frac{1}{4} \text{cycles/instruction}} = 400 \text{ MIPS}$$

The processor can launch two floating point instructions (one add and one multiply) on each clock cycle. This is two floating point operations per clock cycle or

$$\frac{100 \times 1{,}000{,}000 \text{ cycles/second}}{\frac{1}{2} \text{cycles/floating point result}} = 200 \text{ MFLOPS}$$

3.5 The Memory Bottleneck

Note that, as the peak performance of the processor increases, the sustained performance also increases, although not as fast.

As soon as the ability to execute multiple floating point operations at each clock cycle was implemented in processors, an interesting phenomenon occurred. This interesting side effect of increasing the MIPS and FLOPS rates is that the execution speed of floating point computations is no longer bound by the speed of the processor. The overwhelming issue in measuring the time to execute a program is the time to stream operands from main memory into the processor. In essence, the processor computes so quickly that the memory systems cannot keep up. This is referred to as the *memory bottleneck*.

Memory Hierarchies

There are actually different kinds of memory. Memory chips come in a range of speeds, ranging from "very fast" to "not so fast." The faster memory chips are more expensive and, if used, are used in smaller quantities in a memory subsystem. Static RAMs, or SRAMs, are relatively fast, but the memory that is most often preferred is Dynamic RAMs, or DRAMs, which are relatively fast and inexpensive. One way fast memory is used is cache memory; caches have a very fast access time and are usually used as a special attached memory that holds data items expected to be fetched and stored often. Caches are discussed in detail later.

Memories of different latency may be layered in a memory system. That is, different kinds of memory may be connected in a hierarchy that ranges from fastest level (the register file in the microprocessor) through one or more levels of caches, one or more levels of main memory, down to the slowest level, such as a disk, as in Figure 3.2. The size of each of these levels is inversely proportional to the cost of the implementation, and this is easily seen: there is a small number of registers, and caches are limited in size when compared to main memory, for example.

Funky Pipeline: Intel's i860

The i860 microprocessor, with over 2.5 million transistors, is a multiple instruction issue processor. The chip has one integer computation unit and two pipelined floating units; one is strictly for addition and the other strictly for multiplication. Integer instructions are pipelined through the fetch-decode-execute-store cycle, allowing the launch of one integer instruction on every clock cycle. Two floating point operations may be initiated at a time, although the multiplier takes two cycles to deliver a single precision result. This means that two integer operations, one floating point multiply operation, and two floating point addition operations may be executed in two cycles, giving an average of two and a half instructions per cycle. The clock rate is 50 MHz, so the effective MIPS rate is 100 MIPS. Because three floating point operations may be performed every two cycles, the chip delivers 75 MFLOPS. The i860 has an 8K byte instruction cache and an 8K byte data cache.

The floating point pipelines on the i860 have the distinction of being *push-pipes*. That means that instead of a timed pipeline that provides a partial result on each clock cycle, the pipeline advances the computation only when an explicit floating point add or multiply instruction *pushes* values through the respective pipes. For example, the result of a floating point addition does not appear in the destination register until a specific number of floating point addition instructions have been executed.

3.5. The Memory Bottleneck

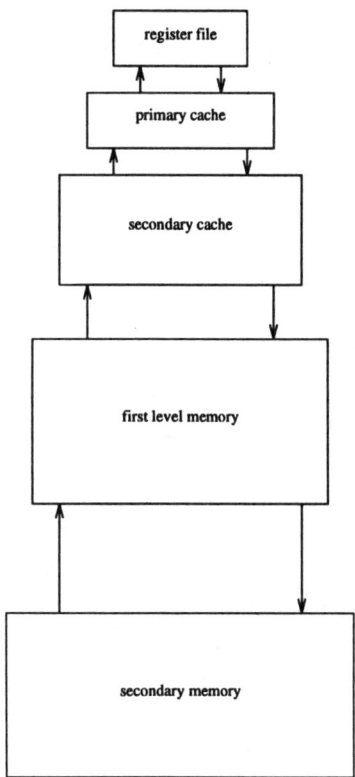

Figure 3.2: Memory hierarchies

Caches

One way to solve the memory bottleneck problem is to add a **cache** to the processor. A cache is a very fast memory that is used as a buffer for data that can be quickly loaded into the CPU. Most RISC and superscalar processors have both data and instruction caches.

Data items in memory are automatically mapped into the cache so that when there is a memory reference in an executed instruction, the cache is checked to see if the referenced item is already in the cache. If it is, the value is quickly retrieved. If not, the data item is fetched into the cache. Depending on the hardware implementation, some surrounding data may also be fetched into the cache, based on the idea that if one data item is used, perhaps some data near by might also be used. This chunk of data, referred to as a **cache line**, is the smallest quantity of data that is brought into the cache at any time.

As an example, on some machines a cache line may encompass 32 bytes of memory. Each byte that falls within that range of 32 addresses is mapped to the same cache line. If one memory address is referenced, the whole 32 byte cache line that contains that referenced address is brought into the cache. Cache operation is most often hardware specified, and is not under user control. Because of this, it is often hard to know what data is in the cache.

Bringing Data into the Cache

When data are in the cache, the latency for delivery into the processor is not more than a few clock cycles. However, if data are not in the cache, a significant time penalty is paid to fetch the data from memory. If a user writes a program that often fetches values that are in the cache, the program will run much faster than if the program fetches values that are not in the cache. But how can a user write a program that uses data in the cache if what is in the cache is unknown?

One way is to make use of **prefetch** instructions that are available in a number of processor instruction sets. A prefetch instruction requests a load from memory ahead of the time that the data will be used. This allows computations to be overlapped with the memory delay.

Another way is to take advantage of knowledge about the layout of data and the fact that when a memory address is referenced and that element is

3.5. The Memory Bottleneck

Blinding Speed: Digital's Alpha

In early 1992, Digital Equipment Corporation announced the 21064 Alpha microprocessor. This chip, which runs at a blinding 150 MHz, is the first of a family of superscalar, superpipelined high performance microprocessors. The Alpha is a multiple instruction issue processor, with four independent functional units: an integer unit, a fully pipelined floating point unit, a load/store unit, and a separate branch unit.

The Alpha has a true 64-bit RISC architecture. The Alpha architecture, which is destined to replace the VAX architecture as Digital's primary machine architecture, provides flexibility by allowing a user to run any of an assortment of operating systems, most notably VMS and OSF/1. One of the most interesting features of the Alpha is that its architecture does not enforce strict read/write ordering between multiple processors; this allows the chip to be easily integrated into a multiprocessor architecture. This is evidenced by Cray's choice of the Alpha as its node microprocessor for its T3D Massively Parallel Processor computer.

Hot Chip: Intel's Pentium

The Pentium is Intel's "fence-sitting" microprocessor. Successor to Intel's x86 series, it bears resemblance to a RISC microprocessor in a number of ways, such as its 8K instruction cache, instruction prefetching, and its capacity for issuing multiple instructions on each processor cycle. On the other side of the fence, the Pentium is still regarded as a CISC processor; it is similar to Intel's earlier 486 CISC processor in design.

The Pentium is hot is more than one way: it is reported[a] that the chip has a maximum power dissipation of 16 watts when run at 66MHz, which is four times the power dissipation of the 486.

---

[a]Microprocessor Report, **7.4**

not in the cache, the address's full cache line is loaded. Then, if the program references any other addresses whose data have been loaded into the same cache line, the data are in the cache and can be streamed into the CPU quickly. This is the kind of transformation a user would like a compiler to perform automatically.

An Example

The best way to explain how to take advantage of knowledge of layout is to show how different implementations of an algorithm interact with the cache. Consider the following Fortran program fragment that implements array addition:

```
REAL A(100, 300), B(100, 300), C(100, 300)
INTEGER I, J

DO I = 1, 100, 1
   DO J = 1, 300, 1
      A(I, J) = B(I, J) + C(I, J)
   ENDDO
ENDDO
```

This code fragment iterates over each row, and within each row it walks through each column, adding the corresponding elements of arrays B and C and storing the result into the corresponding element of array A. In Fortran, arrays are stored in column-major order. Elements of an entire column of the array are stored in consecutive memory locations so that the array element A(1,1) is right next to array element A(2,1). Because of this axis ordering, the preceding implementation uses the cache in a very inefficient way.

3.5. The Memory Bottleneck

> Many memory addresses are mapped into a small number of addresses in a cache. When the cache is full and a new memory reference does not map into the cache, this cache miss is remedied by bringing the referenced memory line into the cache. Yet, if the cache is full, the new cache line must replace a line that already is mapped into the cache. An algorithm, called a *cache replacement strategy* must be implemented to consult when determining which cache line is to be "kicked out" of the cache. Often the algorithm used is the Least Recently Used (or LRU) algorithm. This algorithm selects the cache line that has been referenced least recently as the cache line to be replaced.

Let's use the following assumptions:

- The program runs on a processor with an 8K data cache.

- Each REAL element takes up 4 bytes, and each array contains 30,000 elements, so each array occupies 120,000 bytes of memory.

- A 16 byte cache line is loaded from main memory into the cache whenever any byte in that cache line is fetched.

- An element that is written, but not fetched, need not be in the cache.

- The cache replacement strategy is Least Recently Used (**LRU**, i.e., when the cache is full and a cache line needs to be overwritten, the least recently used cache line is chosen).

- Each array begins at an address that is an exact multiple of 16.

The first time through these loops, the value for I is 1 and the value for J is 1. The code fetches the array value B(1,1), which forces a load of the cache line that array element occupies into the cache. Because the array is laid out in column-major order, the elements loaded are B(1,1), B(2,1), B(3,1), and B(4,1). The corresponding elements of C are also loaded into the cache when C(1,1) is fetched. Since the inner loop iterates over the columns, the next time through the column index J will have the value 2, indicating a fetch of the array elements B(1,2) and C(1,2). These elements will not be in the cache, and fetching them will force a load of another two cache lines.

By the completion of the first execution of the inner loop, two cache lines of four elements each have been loaded 300 times. This is equivalent to 300 elements per array × 2 arrays × 4 bytes per element × 4 elements per cache line, or 9600 bytes that had to be loaded into the cache. Since the cache holds only 8192 bytes, some of the loaded elements had to have been overwritten. The least recently used cache lines were the ones loaded the first few iterations of the inner loop. Therefore, when the next iteration of the outer loop begins, and I is 2, the array elements B(2,1) and C(2,1) are no longer sitting in the cache! This means that two cache lines will be loaded *in each iteration of the inner loop.*

To make the execution more cache efficient, notice that each cache line load brings four elements from the same column into the cache. Since the programmer will know that those elements are in the cache, why not take advantage of that knowledge? To do this, the programmer needs only to interchange the loops. That is, iterate over the columns in the outer loop instead of the inner loop:

```
REAL A(100, 300), B(100, 300), C(100, 300)
INTEGER I, J

DO J = 1, 300, 1
   DO I = 1, 100, 1
      A(I, J) = B(I, J) + C(I, J)
   ENDDO
ENDDO
```

In this case each element is loaded into the cache once, and the loaded elements are used right away.

Interleaved Memory

> The **bandwidth** of a data pathway is a measurement of the capacity of the pathway.

One way to widen the memory bandwidth is to use multiple memory banks that can operate in parallel. Addresses can then be interleaved, or

3.5. The Memory Bottleneck

> **Peace Pact: PowerPC**
>
> IBM and Apple may seem to be strange bedfellows, but the two companies teamed up with Motorola to design and build a new RISC microprocessor: the PowerPC. The first chip in the series, the PowerPC 601, was successfully fabricated in the Fall of 1992. The architecture is based on the processor from IBM's successful RS/6000 workstation, the RIOS chip.
>
> The PowerPC 601 contains 2.8 million transistors, and implementations can be offered to run either at 50 MHz or at 66MHz. The 601 contains four pipelines: a load/store pipeline, an integer pipeline, a floating point pipeline, and a branch pipeline; the superscalar 601 allows for multiple instruction issue. Like the i860, the floating point unit allows for simultaneous multiplication and addition.
>
> The PowerPC 601 is the first in the series; the follow-ons, the 604 and the high performance 620, are expected to be popular chips, as Apple migrates its Macintosh series of personal computers and workstations to use RISC technology.

allocated to different memory banks in a modulo fashion. That is, multiple banks of memory are used to make up the entire address space. Each consecutive address is assigned on a round-robin basis to a specific memory bank, so that, for example, if memory address i is assigned to memory bank 10, then memory address $i+1$ is assigned to memory bank 11, and so on. With interleaved memory, when two consecutive addresses are fetched, the hardware can begin loading values from the different memory banks in parallel; the two values can be delivered into registers (or the cache) in the same amount of time as loading a single value.

DRAM Page Optimization

On a finer level, there are issues regarding the accessing of memory at the hardware level within the memory chip itself. As an example, consider the use of DRAM chips. Internal to the DRAM chip, when an address is referenced, the memory page that contains the referenced address is loaded into a buffer local to the DRAM. If a subsequent reference is an address that maps to the same DRAM page, the value can be delivered more quickly, since the DRAM page has already been loaded into the local buffer. On the other hand, if the next referenced address does not fall within the same DRAM page, then the local buffer must be filled with the page that holds the new reference. This is called a *DRAM page fault.* The time to fill the buffer with the page is incorporated into the time to fetch that referenced value from memory.

This indicates that in a system using DRAM memory, referencing "near" addresses in sequence (that is, addresses that fall within the same DRAM page) will be faster than referencing "far" addresses (or addresses that map into different DRAM pages), since once the DRAM's local buffer is filled with a specific page, fetching values from that page may be done without reloading the page. For example, consider this simple vector addition loop on a system where each DRAM page takes up 1024 bytes:

```
REAL A(256), B(256), C(256)
INTEGER I
DO I = 1, 256
   A(I) = B(I) + C(I)
ENDDO
```

Since the element size in each of the arrays is 4 bytes, each array takes up 1024 bytes. Each iteration of the loop requires a fetch of an element of B and an element of C, and a store to an element of A. We know that because the page size is 1024 bytes, the corresponding indexed elements of A, B, and C are mapped to different DRAM pages. If a value of B is fetched and, subsequently, the corresponding indexed value of C is fetched, each reference will force a DRAM page fault. Similarly, the corresponding index into A being stored immediately following the fetches of elements from B and C will also force a DRAM page fault. If a DRAM page fault adds 10 cycles to the time of referencing a value in memory, then each array reference wil cost an additional 10 cycles, or an extra 30 cycles per loop iteration. Multiplying 30 by 256, the number of iterations, means that there is an extra 7680 cycles in the execution of this loop.

How can this delay be minimized? Sometimes a compiler is "smart" enough to figure out a way to reference the arrays without alternating between DRAM pages. Even if not, sometimes the compiler can determine that certain values may be held in registers; if so, then one way that the programmer could try to help the situation is to load values in "streams." For example, the previous loop could be rewritten as this:

3.6. Conclusion

```
REAL A(256), B(256), C(256)
INTEGER T1, T2, T3, T4
INTEGER S1, S2, S3, S4
INTEGER I

DO I = 1, 256, 4
   T1 = B(I)
   T2 = B(I+1)
   T3 = B(I+2)
   T4 = B(I+3)

   S1 = C(I)
   S2 = C(I+1)
   S3 = C(I+2)
   S4 = C(I+3)

   T1 = T1 + S1
   T2 = T2 + S2
   T3 = T3 + S3
   T4 = T4 + S4

   A(I) = T1
   A(I+1) = T2
   A(I+2) = T3
   A(I+3) = T4
ENDDO
```

In this loop, four values from B and C are read at a time, and four results are stored to A at a time. Instead of looping 256 iterations, there are only 64 iterations. In each iteration, there are still three DRAM page faults, each one costing 10 cycles, but the total extra cost is 30×64, or 1920 extra cycles. This is one-fourth the extra time spent in the first implementation.

3.6 Conclusion

As can be seen, the advance in design technology for microprocessors is creating an environment where high performance systems will be sitting on the desktop, as well as provide powerful node processing for multiple processor systems. What is the projected hybrid solution? Superfast microprocessor used as workstations on the desktop during the daytime, but networked together to form scalable multiprocessor systems for high performance as well. The workstation farm consisting of a fast network connecting heterogeneous microprocessor-based workstations may soon replace the large supercomputer as the computation resource of choice. The individual workstations in the cluster can provide for the individual needs as a desktop resource, while larger problems can take advantage of the collective unused processor power.

Chapter 4

Topological Issues

In any system with multiple processing units, there must be some pathway for those processing units to communicate. Whether we talk about a loosely coupled local area network or a high speed massively parallel processing (MPP) system, the processing elements are connected in a **network**.

Before we can talk about different kinds of multiple processor systems, it would be enlightening to examine the nature of networks. We will look into different kinds of network attributes, such as

- *Connectivity.* This is the nature of the connections in the system. For example, networks can be *fully connected*, where every node is connected to every other node, or *partially connected*, where some of the nodes are connected to some other set of nodes.

- *Topology.* The topology of a network is the mapping by which the nodes are connected.

- *Latency.* Latency is the amount of time it takes for a message to traverse the network.

- *Bandwidth.* Bandwidth is the capacity of the network in number of bytes per time period. If a network is compared to a river, the bandwidth is equivalent to the amount of water that can travel along the river at any time.

- *Functionality.* Some networks have additional embedded functions, such as combining messages. For example, a network may have send-with-operation functions that can combine all elements in a network

46   Chapter 4. Topological Issues

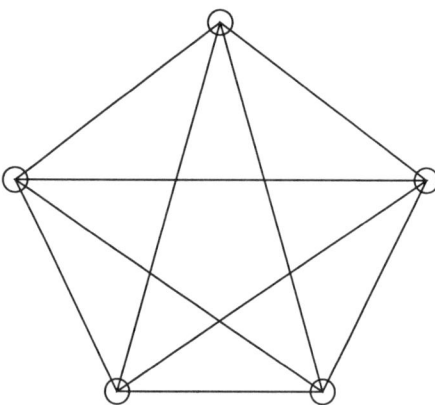

Figure 4.1: A fully connected graph with five vertices

under the specified operation. Different operations may be specified, such as addition. Combining sends are used, among other things, for parallel prefix operations.

4.1 Connectivity

To understand the way networks work, some definitions are useful. Formally, a *graph* is a tuple (**V**, **E**) consisting of *vertices* and *edges*. Edges are links that connect the vertices in the graph. A graph is said to be *fully connected* when there is an edge connecting all pairs of vertices in the graph, as in Figure 4.1. A graph is said to be *partially connected* if not all the pairs of vertices are directly connected, as in Figure 4.2.

In a computer network, the vertices correspond to processor nodes in the network and the edges correspond to connections between those nodes. We will look at some of the different ways to achieve different levels of connectivity, but it is important to understand how nodes and wires are configured in a system through the use of switches.

4.2 Switches

A network may be configured using **switches** that can reroute a message along a choice of paths. Using a combination of switches, the network can be

4.2. Switches

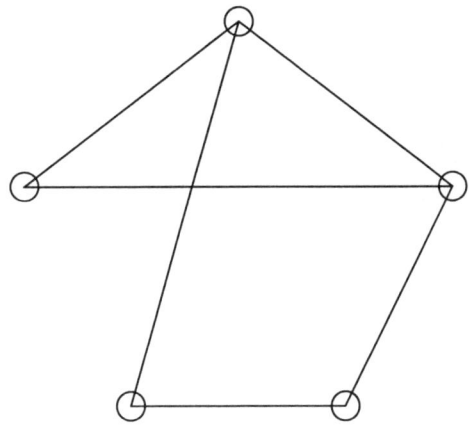

Figure 4.2: A partially connected graph

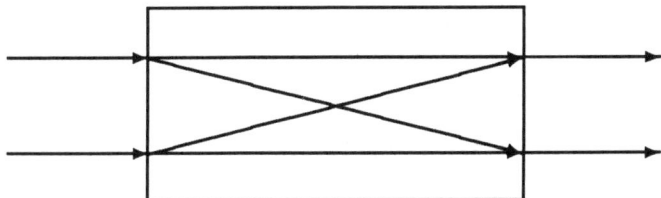

Figure 4.3: A two-by-two switch

constructed such that the amount of time for a node in an N-node network to send a message to any other node in the network is on the order of $ln(N)$. An example of a logarithmic network can be built using a butterfly switch. Figure 4.3 shows a picture of a single two-by-two switch and how that switch is used to build a logarithmic network. A message passing through a two-by-two switch can either be routed along the top path or the bottom path, as in Figure 4.4.

By using a two-by-two switch, four nodes may be connected together. Switches may be connected together to form simple multistage switching networks. For example, Figure 4.5 shows an Omega network, where the switches are connected in a configuration referred to as a perfect shuffle.

Each node in the network is ordered, and that order is translated into

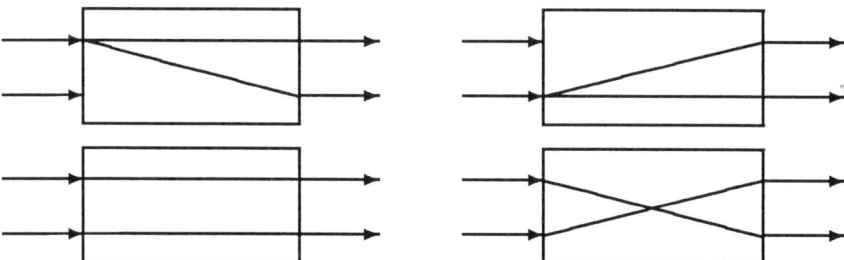

Figure 4.4: Data paths through a two-by-two switch

its corresponding bit string. When a message is sent from one node in the network to another, it is tagged with the destination node's bit string. The way messages are routed in an Omega network is that, at each step in the path, the switch strips off the first bit of the destination bit string. If that bit is a "0," then the message is routed through the top connection in the switch; if the bit is a "1," direct the message through the bottom half of the switch. The message is sent along with the destination bit string stripped of the examined bit, to be examined at the next stage in the network.

The Omega network is a simple network, which may *block* or stall messages, in the network when a pathway is being used. Other switch/network connectivities can overcome this blocking; these are referred to as *nonblocking* networks. Examples of these are Benes networks and full-connection crossbars.

4.3 Topologies and Routing

Linear Networks and Rings

A linear network is a collection of nodes connected in a one-dimensional array. Except for the nodes on the ends, each node has a direct connection to two neighbors. The nodes on the end are connected only to one neighbor. A good example of a linear network is a wire ethernet. Usually, nodes are connected to a single wire through which communication takes place. If the two end nodes are connected, the resulting network is a ring (see Figure 4.6).

A ring network consists of a connectivity to which all the processors are

4.3. Topologies and Routing

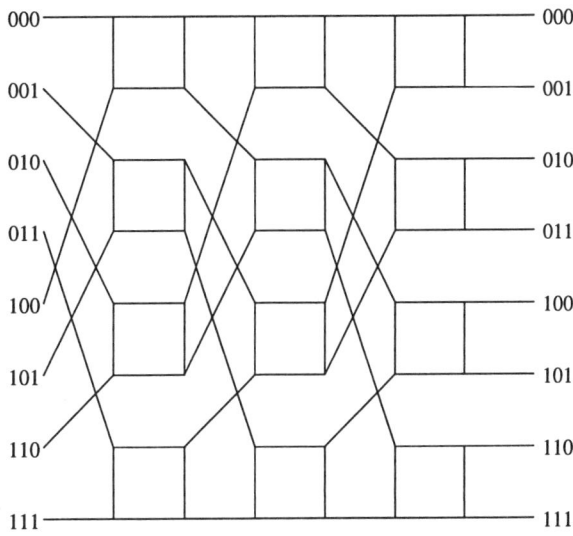

Figure 4.5: Omega network

attached. Processors connected in a ring network can inject messages into the network in a number of different ways, but in high performance MPP machines, a preferred method is through the use of message slots.

The network can be viewed as a chain of "boxes" into which messages are either placed or removed. At each time quantum, the chain shifts along the ring one step. At this point, the nodes on the network can examine their corresponding boxes to see if a message needs to be withdrawn, or a node may insert a message into an empty box.

A ring network has the advantage of yielding high connectivity with a small number of physical connections. When using very high speed wires, the effect of the ring is that of a fully connected graph without the overhead of actual wire connections between all pairs of nodes.

Hypercube

An N-dimensional hypercube is a network connectivity scheme over 2^N nodes are connected such that each node in the network is directly connected to N neighbors. For example, a network taking the geometrical shape we

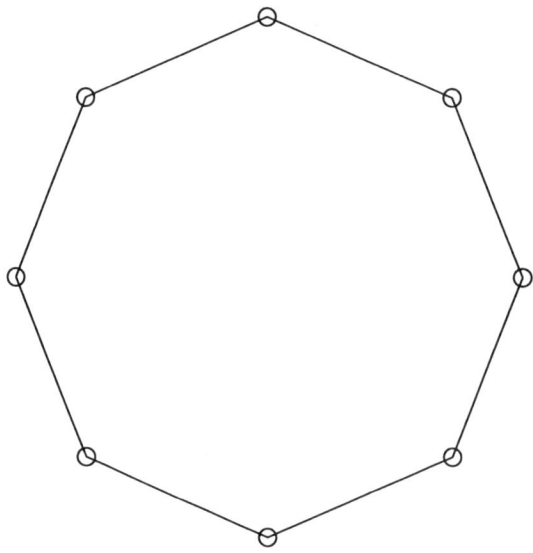

Figure 4.6: Ring network

refer to as a cube is an example of a three-dimensional hypercube; each node in the network is connected to three neighbors. Figure 4.7 contains some examples of low order hypercubes.

The benefit of a hypercube is in the degree of connectivity and the simplicity of mapping addresses. Each node in the hypercube network is ordered, and then its ordering is identified with a label that consists of a set of individual bits. An arbitrary node $node_i$ is connected to all nodes whose labels differ from $node_i$'s label in a single bit position. Figure 4.8 shows three- and four-dimensional hypercubes.

For example, consider a five-dimensional hypercube. This hypercube would consist of 2^5 nodes, or 32 nodes. Node 22 would carry the bit label

4.3. Topologies and Routing

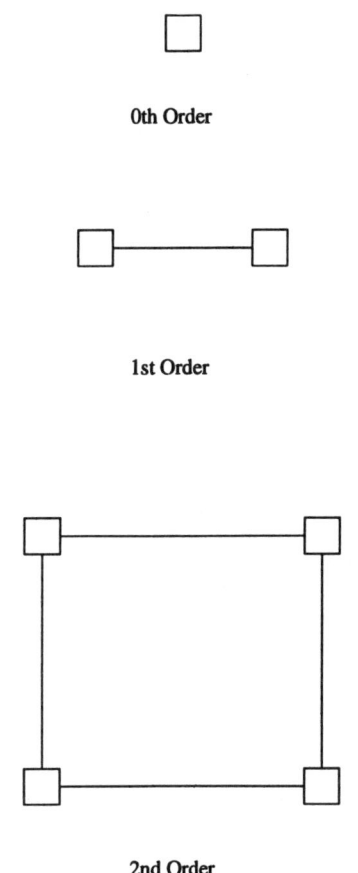

Figure 4.7: Order 0, 1, and 2 hypercubes

52   Chapter 4. Topological Issues

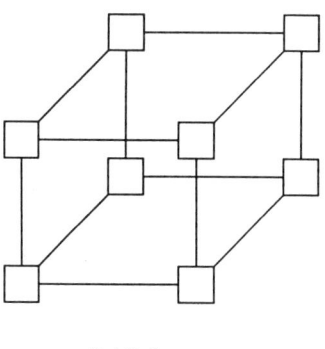

3rd Order

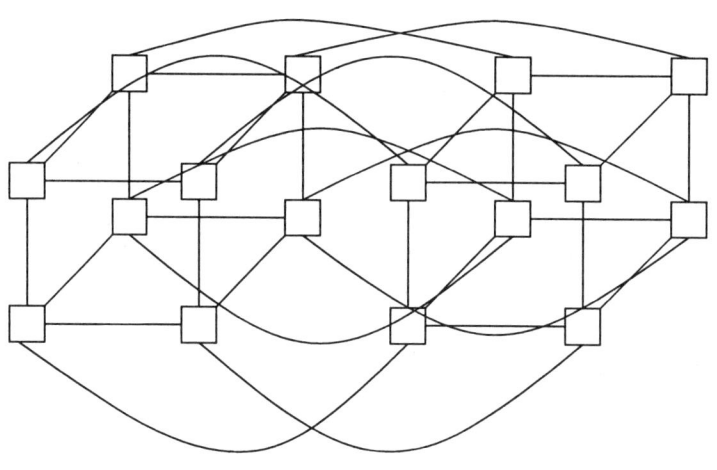

4th Order

Figure 4.8: Order 3 and 4 hypercubes

4.3. Topologies and Routing

10110. Node 22 is directly connected to nodes whose labels differ from node 22's label by a single bit, i.e., the nodes with these labels: **00110** (node 6), **11110** (node 31), **10010** (node 18), **10100** (node 20), and **10111** (node 23).

To map a pathway for a message from one node in the network to another, the network effectively constructs a sequence of bit strings that sequentially differ in one bit until the destination label has been formed. Because each bit string in the sequence represents a node in the network that is a neighbor of the node represented by the preceding bit string, this sequence effectively defines a specific route for the message.

As an example, consider routing a message from a node with the label **10110** to a node with the label **01101** in a five-dimensional hypercube. Once possible sequence is **10110, 00110, 01110, 01100, 01101.** The message can be sent along the network using this sequence as a route. Of course, as long as the message is tagged with its destination label, the message can be sent one node at a time, each node figuring out the next bit to change in the label.

Fat-Tree Network

A fat-tree network is a tree-structured network in which all the processing nodes and devices are located at the leaves of the tree. As the hierarchy levels ascend in the tree, the channel capacitites increase, thereby increasing the communication bandwidth at higher levels in the tree. Because of this hierarchical nature, a machine using a fat-tree network can easily be broken up into different size partitions that do not interfere with each other. An example of a fat-tree can be found in Figure 4.9.[1]

---

[1] For a more detailed description of fat-trees, see [37].

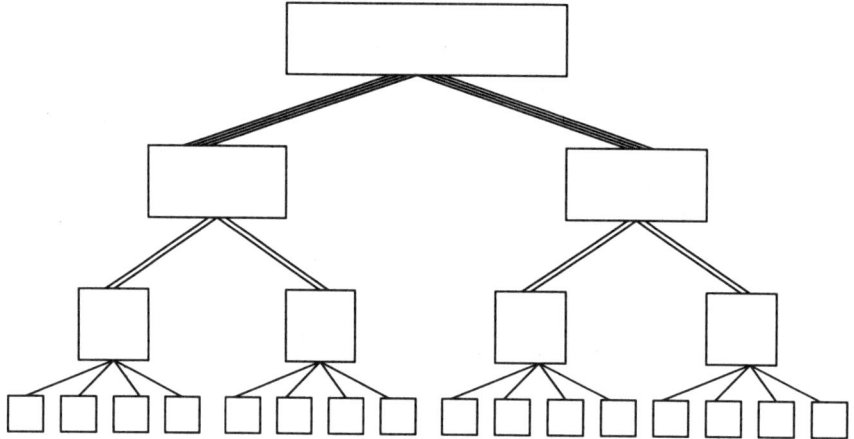

Figure 4.9: A fat-tree network

Mesh

A mesh network connects processing nodes in a Cartesian grid. In a two-dimensional mesh, all the nodes are configured in a two-dimensional grid, with each node connected to its immediate neighbors in the grid. This implies that every interior node is connected to four neighbors, while edge nodes may be connected to fewer. A mesh may be *toroidal*, i.e., the edges may also be "wrapped around" and nodes on the edges connected to each other. Figure 4.10 shows an example of a two-dimensional mesh.

A three-dimensional mesh adapts a collection of two-dimensional meshes to a third dimension. Figure 4.11 shows an example of a three-dimensional mesh. The 3-D mesh takes the topography of a 2-D mesh and "repeats" the pattern along a new dimension. A mesh is said to be *toroidal* when the edges are "wrapped around" and connected to give a round or spherical surface. Note that, in Figure 4.11, the nodes of the front plane are directly connected to the nodes on the final plane.

Meshes are used because many applications map well to this topology. For example, computational chemistry applications compute the effects of molecules in motion. The molecules represented in one node on the network usually will "move" only to adjoining nodes, not to any arbitrary location in the network.

4.4. Network Functionality

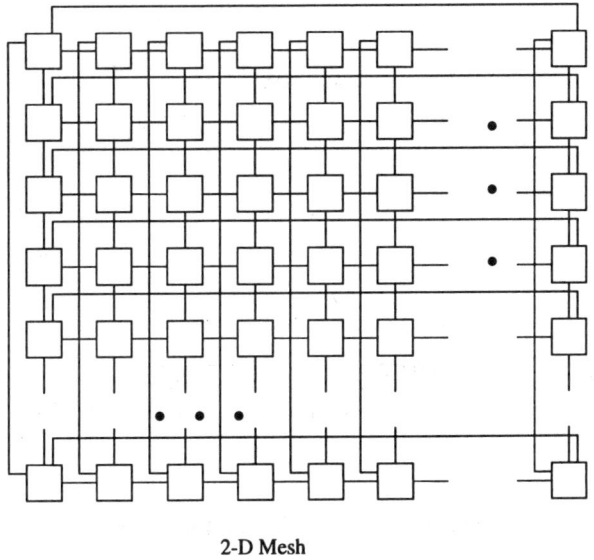

2-D Mesh

Figure 4.10: Two-dimensional mesh

4.4 Network Functionality

As mentioned earlier, some networks may have additional functions implemented as part of the network functionality. One class of these functions is *combining*. Combining messages using one of a set of operations is a way to perform computation over a collection of operands while they are traveling through the network. For example, consider a network that provides a SEND-with-ADD combining operation. This combining operation will add the elements that are sent along the network, until the reduced result arrives at the final destination. The resulting value is the summation of the sent values. This implements a SUM reduction over the elements sent.

Another network function is *hardware synchronization*. At certain times during the execution of an application, it may be necessary for all the executing nodes to indicate to each other that they have reached a specific point in the program. This "meeting place" is called a *synchronization point* or, if all nodes participate, a *barrier synchronization*, and the functionality is often offered as part of the network. One way to implement a synchronization using the network is through the use of a global-AND. Each node indicates

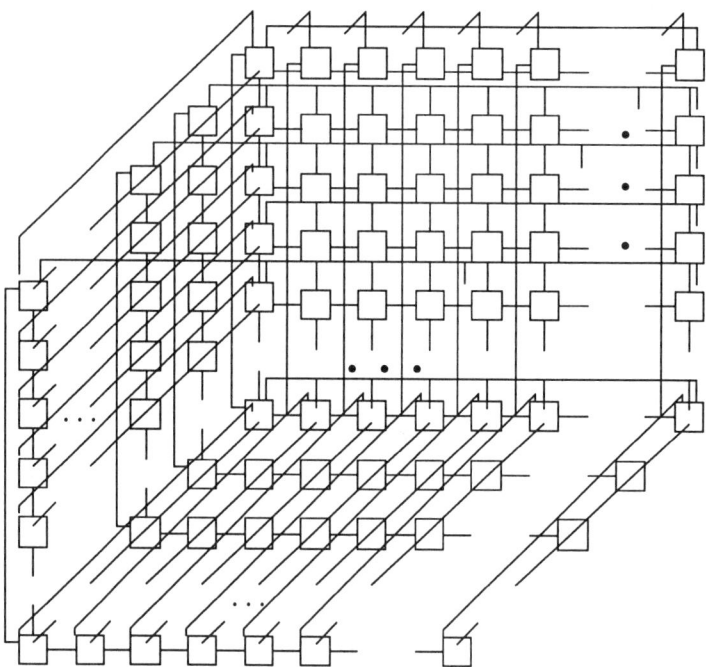

Figure 4.11: Three-dimensional mesh

4.5. New Trends in Communications 57

that it has reached the synchronization point by setting a specific network-visible bit to 1. Until all bits are set to 1, the global-AND will return 0; as soon as all the bits have been set, the global-AND will then return a 1, indicating that all nodes have reached that point in their execution.

4.5 New Trends in Communications

Networks are composed of transmission media (usually wires) that are used for the transfer of data across distances. As the amount of information that flows along different networks explodes, it is becoming evident that the bandwidth of these networks is insufficient to carry the load. With the need for data transfers increasing (for example, due to the initiation of the information superhighway or for multimedia interfaces such as "video-on-demand"), there will be a need for greater network bandwidth.

Asynchronous Transfer Mode

One of the mechanisms that is being investigated for increasing network bandwidth is changing from using the traditional Synchronous Transfer Mode, or **STM**, to an Asynchronous Transfer Mode, or **ATM**. To understand the benefits of ATM, a brief explanation of STM is in order.

Synchronous Transfer Mode is a switched networking mechanism that allocates and reserves bandwidth of a connection between two endpoints for the duration of a communication sequence. The bandwidth of the communication link is divided into *time slots* into which messages are placed by the sender and removed by the receiver. There is a fixed number of time slots, ordered from 1 to some upper bound. The division of the bandwidth cycles; after the time slot labeled with the upper bound passes, the cycle begins again with the first time slot.

For any particular pair of endpoints, a particular labeled slot is allocated for communication. The two endpoints coordinate by reading or writing into the assigned time slot; therefore, if a message takes up more than one time slot, the two endpoints must wait for the time slots to cycle around to continue the communication. On the other hand, if there is time when the two endpoints are not communicating, the time slots are left empty.

The fact that often the time slots cycle without being used is a significant waste of bandwidth. This has prompted the development of an asynchronous mode, where instead of allocating a particular time slot for the duration of communication, each message is of fixed size and contains a connection identifier that is used to route the message along the way to its destination. In this way, network bandwidth can be allocated on a more demand-driven basis.

An ATM message is of fixed size. Each message contains information about its destination, as encompassed by a virtual circuit identifier, which identifies the destination of the message, as well as up to 48 bytes of *payload*, or message. It is up to the application using ATM to provide mapping information for reconstructing large messages broken up into smaller "chunks." The virtual circuit interface, or VCI, is used as a tag for a destination, but each node in the network may locally remap a VCI via an entry in a connection table.

ATM is designed to provide high bandwidth across networks and should prove useful when building integrated voice and data networks, high bandwidth connections for workstations, or even multimedia applications. ATM is not yet available commercially, but should be by the mid-1990s.

Part III

Multiple Processor Architectures

Each of the four chapters in this part covers a distinct way of connecting processing power together to form a high performance machine. The first chapter talks about vector processor machines, those machines designed to perform operations on large vector operands. The next chapter covers multiple processor architectures, ranging from closely knit networks of cooperating processors to loosely coupled shared-bus machines. The third chapter is a discussion of the Collection of Workstations,or as it is alternatively known, the Workstation Farm. This consists of a collection of high performance workstations connected via a network scheme that creates a system users can use as either single node workstations or as a more powerful multiple processor system. The last chapter discusses issues regarding I/O (input and output).

Chapter 5

Vector Processors

As discussed in Chapter 2, supercomputers were first developed as workhorses for array and matrix computations. These computers are built using pipelined vector processors or with attached array processors. There are variants on these themes, such as systolic arrays. This chapter will discuss different methods used for vector processing and will describe the actual implementations. Speedup in these kinds of machines is achieved through parallelism. The parallelism may either be *temporal* (i.e., pertaining to time) or *spatial* (i.e., pertaining to space).

The architecture descriptions in this chapter are limited to those specifically designed for vector operations. This includes vector processors, attached array processors, and SIMD (single instruction, multiple data) machines. The following chapter will cover more general multiple processor machines, such as Shared Memory machines, and Scalable High Performance machines.

5.1 Pipelined Supercomputers

Pipelined architectures are designed to allow overlapping of a number of different phases of a vector operation to achieve vector parallelism. The idea of a pipelined computer conjures up images of a manufacturing assembly line, with unfinished products moving down the line, constantly being modified until complete products emerge at the end of the line. A pipeline architecture is designed to allow overlapping of partial computations over a sequence of operands. Overlapping steps of a number of different computations is an example of *temporal parallelism*. Through the use of multiple functional units inside the Arithmetic/Logical Unit (ALU), partial results of many sets of operands can be computed at the same time.

Let's take a look at our vector operation example from Chapter 2:

```
A(1:128) = X*B(1:128) + C(1:128)
```

In a pipeline architecture, a number of sets of operations would be partially computed simultaneously in the different functional units.

The actual action of a pipeline machine is first to "fill" the pipes with values. Once all the pipes are full, they can all compute their partial values at the same time. As soon as the stream of inputs has been completely eaten up, the pipes "drain," pumping out the results until they are clear. Given a pipelined machine with three memory units, an addition unit, and a multiplication unit, our vector example from before would be executed in the pipeline in this sequence:

1. Fill Stage

    - Load X
    - Load B(1)
    - Load C(1)

2. Fill Stage

    - T1 = X * B(1)
    - Load B(2)
    - Load C(2)

3. Fill Stage

    - T2 = T1 + C(1)
    - T1 = X * B(2)
    - Load B(3)
    - Load C(3)
    - initialize counter i to 1

4. Loop Stage

5.1. Pipelined Supercomputers

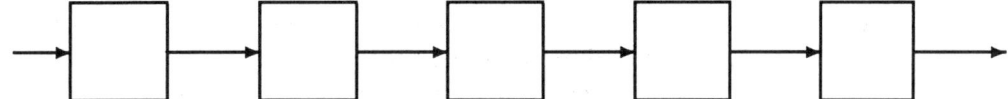

Multiple Stage Pipeline

Figure 5.1: Partial results propagate through the pipeline

- Store T2 into A(i)
- T2 = T1 + C(i+1)
- T1 = X * B(i+2)
- Load B(i+3)
- Load C(i+3)
- increment i
- if i < 126, loop again

5. Drain Stage

- Store T2 into A(126)
- T2 = T1 + C(127)
- T1 = X * B(128)

6. Drain Stage

- Store T2 into A(127)
- T2 = T1 + C(128)

7. Drain Stage

- Store T2 into A(128)

Because the effects of pipelining overlap the operation of many partial computations, the overall effect is one result being generated each time the pipelines are advanced. If the time to advance a pipeline is a single machine cycle, the machine will achieve a result for almost every cycle (taking into account the fill and drain stages of the pipeline).

5.2 Vector Instructions

Given a processor that can pipeline operations, a user would want to perform operations in a vector fashion. That is, if the goal of a vector supercomputer is to perform array and matrix computations, the system must allow for ease of use. A good way is to provide *vector instructions*, or basic vector operations.

Vector processors contain vector registers, which can hold arrays of up to a specified length. Vector instructions can take one of four forms:

1. $V_i \leftarrow V_j \; op \; V_k$. The instruction takes two operands in vector registers, performs the operation, and places the result in a vector register.

2. $V_i \leftarrow V_j \; op \; S_k$. The instruction takes one operand from a vector register and one operand from a scalar register, performs the operation, then places the vector result in a vector register.

3. *Transfer from Memory.* The instruction calls for loading a vector from memory into a vector register.

4. *Transfer to Memory.* The instruction calls for storing a vector value from a vector register into memory.

Some examples of vector operations that are implemented as instructions include standard scalar arithmetic operations, such as addition and multiplication, in a corresponding vector form. Other vector instructions do not correspond to scalar instructions. Some of these instructions are MERGE, which is used for sorting algorithms, GATHER and SCATTER, which are used, respectively, for collecting and disseminating vector values through an indirection vector (see Chapter 2), and some standard matrix operations, such as DOTPRODUCT (the matrix dot-product operation) and MATMUL (standard matrix multiply).

5.3 Early Pipelined Computers: Examples

TI-ASC

The Advanced Scientific Computer (ASC) from Texas Instruments, was an early entry in the supercomputer market. The ASC, introduced in 1972, contains up to four arithmetic pipelines configured as an arithmetic unit, or AU. Each pipeline has eight segments, which are bypassed. The AU is combined with a peripheral processing unit (for the operating system) and a memory buffer unit, or MBU. The purpose of the MBU was to allow continuous streaming of data into the AU. These combined components, along with an instruction processing unit (IPU), made up the central processor. The central processor is attached to eight interleaved memory modules. The processor can execute both scalar and vector instructions.[1]

CDC Star-100

The Control Data Corporation was one of the pioneers in high performance computer systems. The CDC models 6600 and 7600 were two early computer systems that made use of additional "peripheral" processors to perform parts of computations.

The Star-100, delivered by Control Data Corporation in 1973, contains two independent processors, each containing pipelined units. In the first processor, there were two pipelines: a floating point addition unit and a floating point multiplication unit. The second processor contains an addition pipeline, a multipurpose pipeline, and some merge pipelines along with a nonpipelined divide unit. The multipurpose pipeline can perform multiplication, division, and square root determination, among other arithmetic and logical operations. The memory is configured as eight groups with four banks in each group. The memory banks are connected to a *stream unit* though a *storage access control unit*. The stream unit contains data buffers for input and output to memory, and this unit controls the continuous streaming of data in and out of the processors.[2]

5.4 Later Pipelined Computers

CRAY-1

The CRAY-1 processor contains twelve independent functional units, all of them pipelined. Three of the pipelines are used for integer operations and

---

[1] Hwang and Briggs, "Computer Architecture and Parallel Processing," pp. 237–243.
[2] Ibid.

three are used for floating point operations. The other pipelines are used for instruction decoding and address calculations. These pipelines range in number of stages from 2 to 14. There is also an 11-stage pipeline for fetching values from memory into registers.

The pipelines of the CRAY-1 allowed for *chaining*, so that the result of one vector operation could be the input to another vector operation. Usually, when one vector instruction uses a vector register stored by a previous vector instruction, the second operation cannot begin until the first operation completes. In fact, as soon as part of the vector register has been stored, the second instruction can be chained, and can therefore begin to operate on the completed part, yielding an additional level of pipelining. Vector operations that use separate functional units can be chained such that the second operation can begin as soon as the first pipelined result is ready from the first operation. This can eliminate the pipeline startup time for the second operation.[3]

CDC Cyber 205

The Cyber 205 contains up to four floating point pipeline units. Each pipeline has different embedded functional units, which, similar to the CRAY-1, are interconnected to allow for accumulation or other combination operations. The Cyber 205, with a four-way interleaved memory, has a much higher memory bandwidth than the CRAY-1, which is needed to efficiently support memory to memory pipeline instructions.[4] While the Cyber 205 has a longer pipeline startup time than the CRAY-1, the Cyber 205 can handle longer vectors than the CRAY-1.

5.5 Attached Processors

Attached processors may take the form of an individual attached computational unit or a collection of individual units configured as an array. The attached processor performs the floating point operations.

In an attached array processor, an array of specialized processing elements, or PEs, networked together, operate under the control of a single control processor. Attached array processors are often built as SIMD, or sin-

---

[3] Almasi/Gottlieb, "Highly Parallel Computing, pg. 312
[4] Hwang and Briggs, "Computer Architecture and Parallel Processing," pp. 283-285.

5.5. Attached Processors

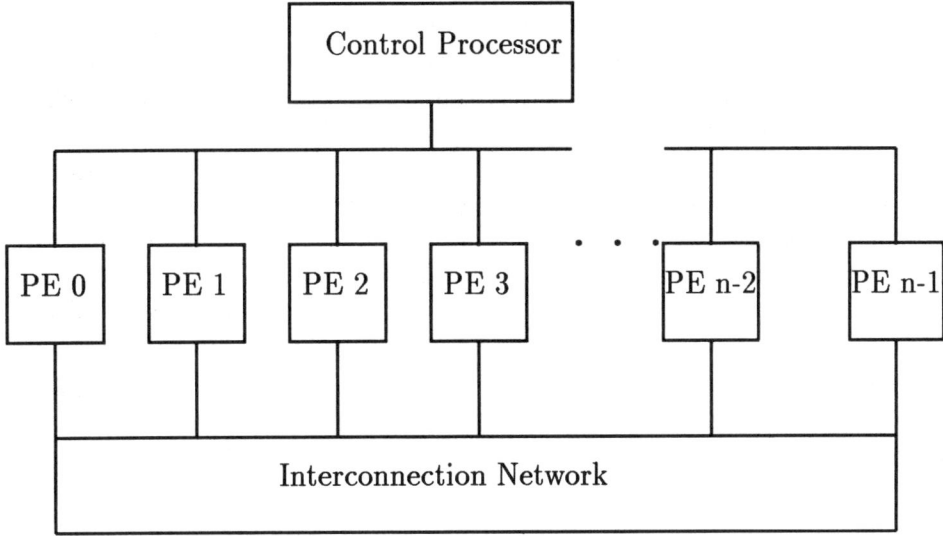

Figure 5.2: SIMD computer: control processor and network of processing elements

gle instruction multiple data machines. The processing elements in a SIMD machine perform the same sequence of operations synchronously over arrays of data.

The control processor is connected to the network of processing elements (see Figure 5.2). A user program resides in the memory of the control processor. Instructions are decoded by the control processor, but the instructions may be either scalar instructions or vector instructions. Scalar instructions are executed by the control processor. Vector instructions, as well as scalar operands to vector instructions, are broadcast to all of the processing elements, where the instructions are executed.[5] Instructions are executed in a "lock-step" fashion. That is, all PEs receive the same instruction from the control processor, and they all execute the same instruction, using data from their own memories. An enabling *masking* scheme is used to signify to each PE whether it is meant to participate in the execution of any particular instruction. In other words, each PE holds a register that can be set to 0 or 1. The register value of 0 indicates that the PE is to remain inactive; a value of 1 tells the PE to participate.

SIMD machines are configured in a way so that vector operands are

---

[5]Ibid., p. 327

accessible by the processing elements. There are two popular memory configurations for this. One is to attach a memory module to each processing element, and the other is to attach a collection of memory modules accessed through the interconnection network. In the first configuration, the data items are distributed across the PEs' memories, allowing for relatively quick access of local data compared to accessing data in another PE's memory. In the second configuration, memory is shared among the processing elements.

Because the processing elements compute the same operation on distinct data elements, SIMD processing is an example of *spatial* parallelism.

ILLIAC IV

One of the first implementations of a SIMD attached processor is the ILLIAC IV computer, which was developed at the University of Illinois. The ILLIAC IV has been called the first supercomputer. The only ILLIAC IV was completed by the Burroughs Corporation in 1972, to be installed at the NASA Ames Research Center.

The ILLIAC IV as implemented is a collection of 64 processing elements attached in a two-dimensional mesh network (see Figure 5.3). The PEs can communicate through a routing mechanism that can transfer a data item from any PE to any other PE. This processor array is attached to a separate control unit using a bus interface. Each PE has its own local memory, and data may be retrieved from PE memory using load and store instructions.

The design called for the use of state of the art technology for the time. The original vision was a set of four quadrants, each of which was to consisted of a control processor and an 8 × 8 processor array. Each processing element was meant to have magnetic thin-film memories. In the four quadrant configuration, the ILLIAC IV was designed to be a 1 GFLOPS machine. The actual implementation of the design for the ILLIAC IV is notorious for a number of reasons. In the final version, only one 8 × 8 quadrant was built, and the highest measured processing rate was 50 MFLOPS, less than 20 percent of the proposed performance. A redesign of the layout did not allow enough space for the original thin-film memories, which had to be replaced by more conventional memory. Last, the ILLIAC IV cost four times the original projected cost.

5.5. Attached Processors

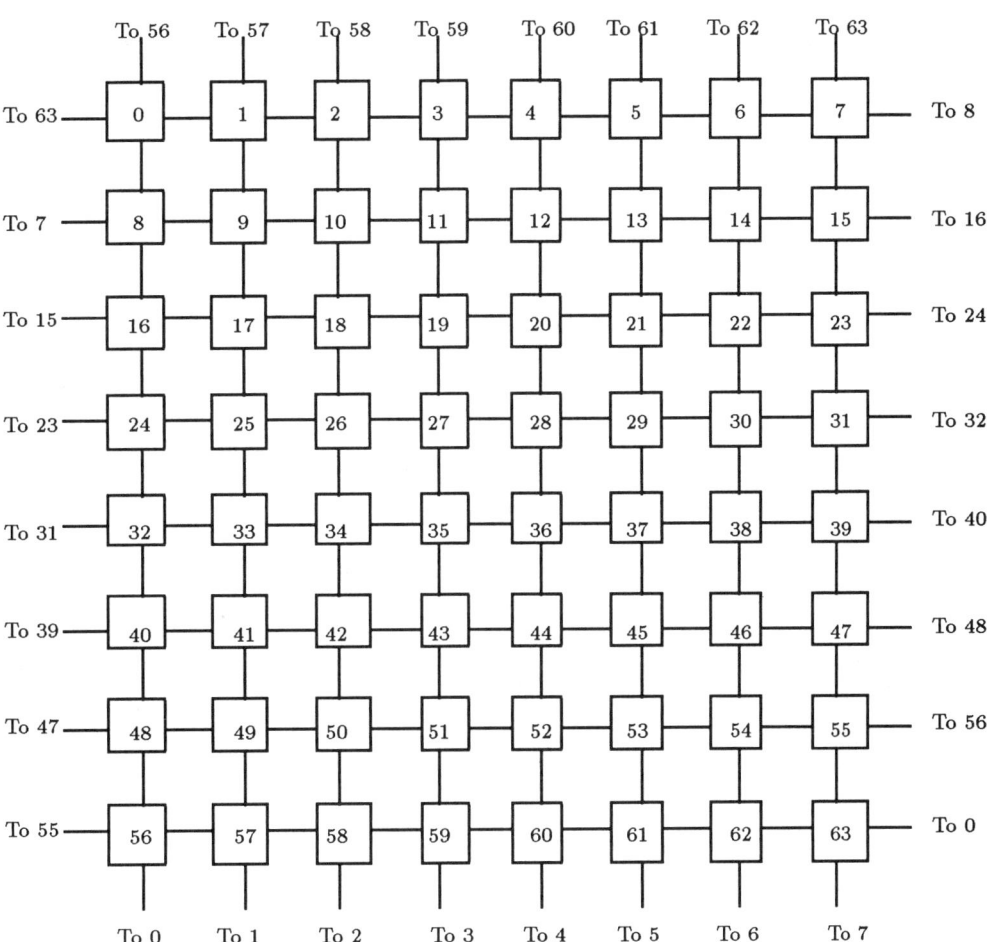

Figure 5.3: The PE mesh on the ILLIAC IV

Burroughs Scientific Processor

The Burroughs Scientific Processor, or the BSP, is an attempt to build on the lessons of the ILLIAC IV, while trying to avoid some of the problems. The BSP is an attached array processor, and unlike the ILLIAC IV, all control functions are decoupled from the computational units. The BSP CPU consists of a control processor, which controls the interface to both the scalar processor and the processor array. The CPU also includes control memory, where the operating system and user program are stored, and a parallel processor controller, used to pass instructions and data to the processor array. The processor array contains 16 processing elements. As opposed to the ILLIAC IV, the BSP's arithmetic elements do not have associated memories; instead, data is stored in a collection of 17 memory modules connected via a fully connected crossbar switch.[6]

MPP

The MPP, or Massively Parallel Processor, was built by Goodyear on contract with NASA. The MPP was designed to be a SIMD processor array for image processing of satellite photos. Similar to the BSP, the design builds on the lessons of the ILLIAC IV, particularly in its use of a two-dimensional mesh network of many processing elements. Each of the processing elements acts as a *bit-slice* processor; i.e., instructions specify bit operations, such as AND and XOR. This is appropriate, considering that these are the operations used to perform image processing. More complex computations can be performed as combinations of bit-slice operations.

The MPP processor array consist of a 128 × 128 two-dimensional grid. The network is similar to that of the ILLIAC IV, although the exact topology is programmable, allowing for either torus shapes along the planes or spiral or cylindrical connections along the processor mesh. Unlike the BSP, each processing element has its own attached memory module.

5.6 New Directions

CRAY Research has advanced vector processors and now offers machines featuring multiple vector processing units. The CRAY C90 series offers up

---
[6]Ibid.

5.6. New Directions

to 16 CPUs, each of which contains two vector pipelines.

Much of the vector processing technology has now been transferred to the microprocessor level, as is discussed in Chapter 3. In fact, much of the technology developed for programming vector machines like the CRAY-1 and the ILLIAC IV has been successfully transferred to superscalar micros.

MPP in the Mainstream

The configurability of the newer SIMD machines and the ability to embed great amounts of logic onto small chips has allowed the evolution of SIMD processor arrays into more powerful massively parallel machines. For example, the processor array computer first manufactured by Thinking Machines Corporation, the Connection Machine-1 (CM-1), is very similar to the Goodyear MPP, although the bit-slice processors are configurable in a more flexible manner. The CM-2, with the incorporation of more powerful floating point processing, was able to compute in both a bitwise and slicewise (i.e., wordwise) model.

In fact, the term MPP has changed from the name of a specific product into one used to describe any computer system consisting of a very large number of processors connected via a high speed, low latency network. A "large" number of processors is considered to be some number between 100 and 1000 processors.

IBM GF-11

The IBM GF-11 is a SIMD computer consisting of 566 processing elements. The GF-11 was designed specifically to solve and verify problems associated with quantum chromodynamics, or QCD. Some of the special statistical operations used in computing QCD are integrated directly into the GF-11 instruction set.

MasPar MP-2

MasPar, one of the early leaders in general purpose massively parallel processor computer systems, built its MP-1 system in the late 1980s. The largest MP-1 configuration delivered a peak performance of 550 64-bit MFLOPS. This system consisted of up to 16,384 RISC microprocessors connected via a two-dimensional torus grid network. Each processor supports high speed near-neighbor communications.

MasPar also provides an execution environment that allows multiple users to use the system simultaneously, as well as a software development environment that eases the way for programmers to build applications. MasPar's current system is called the MP-2. The MP-2 has a peak system performance of up to 2400 64-bit MFLOPS.

Chapter 6

Multiprocessor Machines

Computers constructed of multiple, independent processors allow for a broad view of building applications. Multiple processor machines come in different flavors, although they all share the features of having more than one processor attached to a memory system.

In the previous chapter, we looked at vector computers, where multiple processing units perform the identical operation on different data. Although the single instruction mode of execution is well-suited to many applications, it is constraining when building applications that rely on a larger degree of concurrency. In multiple processor systems, the single instruction constraint may be relaxed, allowing users to build applications under different programming models. To understand the constraining issues, a discussion of parallelism is helpful.

6.1 Parallelism

Vector processors take advantage of the inherent parallelism of specific operations to gain a speedup over scalar processors. In fact, the parallelism achieved using vector processors is only one level of parallelism.

Granularity

Having more than one functional unit in a CPU allows the possibility of having two or more subtasks executing concurrently. The size of the subtasks may be dependent on the configuration of the multiple functional units. In a pipelined vector processor, many subtasks on a vector may be executing concurrently, but each subtask may consist of only a specific operation on operands chosen from a specific pool of operands.

The size of the tasks performed in parallel is referred to as the *granularity*. The small partial computations performed in the vector pipelines are examples of *fine-grain parallelism*. It is possible to imagine applications where the size of subtasks are much larger than those allocated on a vector processor. With a computational unit that comprises more powerful, independent, processors, coarser granularities of parallelism may be programmed.

Different granularities of parallelism can be described using the array addition example:

```
REAL A(1000), B(1000), C(1000)
   .
   .
   .
A(1:1000) = B(1:1000) + C(1:1000)
```

1. *Fine-Grain Parallelism.* In a fine-grain system, the vector operation might be pipelined so that a number of suboperations were being computed simultaneously. The size of each task is partial computation of a single addition.

2. *Medium-Grain Parallelism.* The arrays can be divided into parts, each part allocated to a specific processor. The computation can then be distributed to the processors that own the corresponding parts of the arrays.

3. *Coarse-Grain Parallelism.* The vector addition can be encapsulated as a subtask in its own right, and be allocated to one processor out of a pool of processors. The next vector operation can be allocated to a different processor.

The choice of granularity may be dependent on the hardware configuration of the multiple processor system.

Sources and Levels of Parallelism

Orthogonal to the issue of granularity is the source and level of parallelism. Different levels of concurrency can be determined at different times. Consider these three levels of parallelism:

6.2. Coordination and Synchronization

1. *Instruction Level.* In many cases, instances of parallelism at the instruction level are detected by the hardware.

2. *Loop Level.* A situation where different iterations of a loop may be executed concurrently can be detected by a compiler.

3. *Task Level.* Creating different processes or tasks and allocating them to independent processors may be the result of explicit programming by the user.

6.2 Coordination and Synchronization

Multiple processes, whether they run on a single processor or on a multiple processor machine, often need to communicate. A set of processes that must interact through communication are referred to as *coordinating processes.*

Synchronization is a mechanism for processes to notify each other of having reached a specific point in an execution. Often, synchronization is used to notify others that specific values are up to date.

6.3 Memory Models

It is common to divide the set of multiple processor machines into two classes: shared memory machines and distributed memory machines. Although this categorization may seem appropriate on a hardware level, it is actually possible to simulate a shared memory model using a machine with distributed memory, and conversely, a distributed memory model may be imposed on top of a shared memory machine. A major distinction, according to (Hennesy and Patterson)[1] is the difference in memory access time at each node location. This leads to the idea of a different memory model, the NUMA (non-uniform memory access) model.

Shared Memory

Shared memory systems consist of a number of processors that share a memory subsystem or share a single memory address space (see Figure 6.1). Shared memory computers have in the past been limited to a relatively

---
[1] Hennesy and Patterson, "Computer Architecture A Quantitative Approach," pp. 578-579.

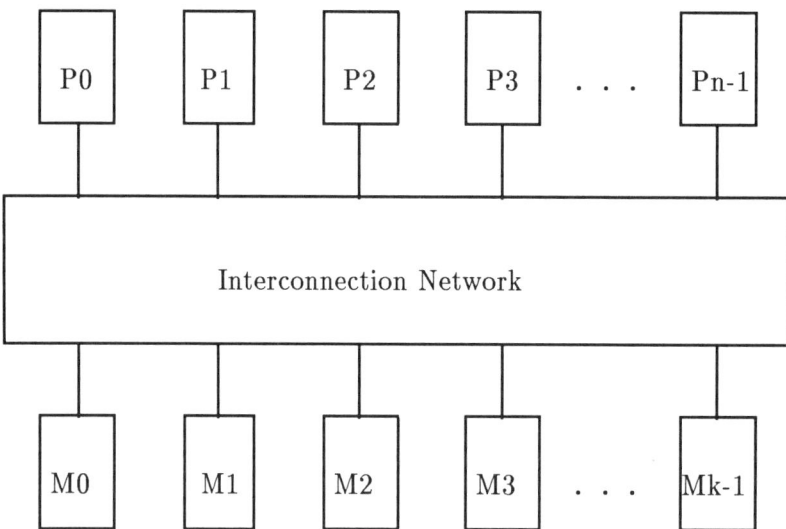

Figure 6.1: Shared memory multiple processor system with n processors and k memories

small number of processors. That is, every memory location in the entire machine is addressable by any processing element in the system. While the memory may be either physically detached or just logically detached from the processing elements, the processing elements in shared memory machines are usually attached to caches. In a shared memory machine, communication and synchronization between processes are done using *shared variables*. The system must provide some kind of mutual exclusion primitives to allow deadlock-free modification to shared variables. Shared address space machines are relatively easy to program, because there are reduced issues of data partitioning or dynamic load balancing.

Two major issues that are currently being addressed by builders of shared memory systems are cache coherence and scalability.

Cache Coherence

One major issue when using caches in a multiple processor machine with a shared memory model is **cache coherence**. Once a memory line has been loaded into a processor's cache, each subsequent time that processor references that memory address, the value is retrieved from the copy in its

6.3. Memory Models

cache. If the actual copy in memory has been modified, (perhaps by another processor), the value in the cache is *invalid*. That is, since the cache held a copy of the previous value, the cache's copy is *incoherent*.

The solution to this is to use a cache coherence protocol. Hardware cache coherence protocols automatically notice that a memory address has been modified. When this happens, and there are existing copies in some of the caches, those cache lines are either *invalidated*, indicating that the copy is incorrect, or *updated* with the correct value.

If the caches are invalidated, this is called a *write-invalidate* policy. The next time the processor accesses that memory address, the invalidation in the cache line is an indication that the value must be reloaded from memory, thereby refreshing the cache copy.

The possible states for a cache line in a write-invalidate scheme are *invalid* (inconsistent with memory), *valid* (consistent with memory), *reserved* (there is only one cache copy which is consistent with memory), and *dirty* (there is only one cache line, and it has been updated more recently than the copy in memory).

Cache coherence becomes more difficult with a larger number of processors. Each processor will have its own first level cache, and processors may be grouped together to share a second level cache. Each time a memory address is written to, the system must invalidate all local cache copies.

As an example of a cache-coherence protocol, the following is a general mechanism for read and write operations using a write-invalidate scheme:

- *Read hit.* If a memory reference is in the cache and it is a valid copy, return the value. No consistency commands need to be issued.

- *Read miss.* A memory reference is not in the cache. If no dirty copy exists, load the (consistent) copy from memory into the cache. If a dirty copy exists, the cache holding the dirty copy updates the requesting cache. Both cache lines are marked as valid, and memory is updated.

- *Write hit.* If a dirty copy exists in the cache, update that dirty copy. If the cache copy is valid, then update the cache, mark the copy as reserved, update memory, and send an invalidate command to the other caches.

- *Write miss.* The cache is updated either with a consistent copy from memory or a dirty copy from another cache. Either way, mark the copy as dirty and send an invalidate consistency command to the other caches.

- *Replacement.* The copy is written out to memory if it is dirty.

If the caches are updated, this is called a *write-update* policy. The following is an example of a write-update cache coherence protocol.

> The possible states for a cache line in a write-update scheme are *valid-exclusive* (consistent with memory), *shared* (there are a number of copies, all of which are consistent with memory) and *dirty* (there is only one cache line, and it has been updated more recently than the copy in memory).

- *Read hit.* If a memory reference is in the cache and it is a valid copy, return the value. No consistency commands need to be issued.

- *Read miss.* A memory reference is not in the cache. If any caches hold a shared copy, the cache line is updated in the cache from another cache. If a dirty copy exists, all caches are updated with the dirty copy. The copy is then marked as shared.

- *Write hit.* If a dirty copy exists in the cache, update that dirty copy. If the cache copy is valid, then update the cache. If the copy is shared, update the cache, then send an update command to the caches holding a shared copy.

- *Write miss.* The cache is updated either with a consistent copy from memory or a dirty copy from another cache. If the copy comes from memory, mark the copy as dirty. If the copy came from another cache, update the copy, send an update consistency command to the other caches and mark the copy as shared.

- *Replacement.* The copy is written out to memory if it is dirty.

Here are two general schemes for cache coherence in a shared memory system:

6.3. Memory Models

- *Snoopy-Based Coherence.* Cache coherence protocols are implemented by hardware issuance of cache consistency commands to all the caches holding a particular cached value. In bus-based networks, it is convenient to broadcast the cache consistency commands to all the caches. It is the responsibility of each cache to listen to, or *snoop* the bus to determine if consistency commands refer to data currently in the cache. An implementation of cache coherence that snoops the bus is called a *snoopy cache protocol*.

- *Directory-Based Coherence.* In a large multiple processor system, using a snoopy-based scheme incurs too much overhead; the cost of broadcasting consistency commands to all nodes on an interconnection network eventually "clogs" it, lowering the efficiency of the network. A solution for this is the *directory* scheme. Instead of broadcasting them over a network, consistency commands are sent only to those caches that hold a copy of a cache line. A directory keeps track of which caches hold copies. When a cache line is updated, the directory is queried, and the appropriate consistency commands are sent directly to the caches with copies.

Scalability

It would be nice if the speedup of a system would stay the same as more processors are integrated into the system. Yet, as more processors (and consequently, caches) are incorporated into a shared memory multiprocessor system, both the cost of accessing memory and the overhead of maintaining consistency grow. In the past, this problem of *scalability* has hampered the development of shared memory systems consisting of more than 32 processors. In fact, when too many processors are added into some systems, the performance may actually degrade due to the increased overhead.

The price/performance of microprocessors is relatively high when compared to that of large scale parallel systems. One current goal of shared memory computer system builders is to design an architecture that can integrate many high performance microprocessors in a scalable fashion with a single, shared address space.

A major issue is efficient cache coherence across multiple levels of a memory hierarchy. It is believed that snoopy-based schemes are not efficient enough for scalable shared memory machines, therefore the directory-based

> ### Scalable Shared Memory: Stanford Dash
>
> The Stanford Dash machine is a research shared memory multiprocessor machine. The name Dash is an abbreviation for directory architecture for shared memory. The Stanford Dash machine is designed as a set of processor clusters connected by an interconnection network. There is a single address space, although the physical memory is distributed with the processors. Each cluster consists of a collection of high performance processors. A number of these clusters are connected to a low latency network.
>
> The Dash machine has a very distinct memory hierarchy. The levels are described in terms of "closeness" to the processor. The *processor level* is the processor's cache. The next level, the *local cluster level*, consists of the caches in other processors in the local cluster. The next level is the *home cluster level*, which contains the cache directory and a certain amount of main memory. The next level is the *remote cluster level*, which consists of processor caches in remote clusters. The Dash architecture also supports prefetch memory operations.
>
> The prototype Dash system was built using a Silicon Graphics Power Station 4D/340 as the base cluster; this machine consists of 4 MIPS R300 processors.

schemes will prevail in these systems. Some research shared memory machines being built are the Stanford Dash machine (described in the boxed text) and the MIT Alewife machine.

Distributed Memory

In a distributed memory system, each processor can address its own set of memory addresses. Data that live in the address space of one processor cannot be written or read by another processor. In a distributed memory system, data are shared through the use of messages. The message passing scheme may be either *synchronous*, where sending nodes and receiving nodes "rendezvous" at the time of message passing, or *asynchronous*, allowing a certain amount of buffering that does not interrupt a sending or receiving process.

6.3. Memory Models

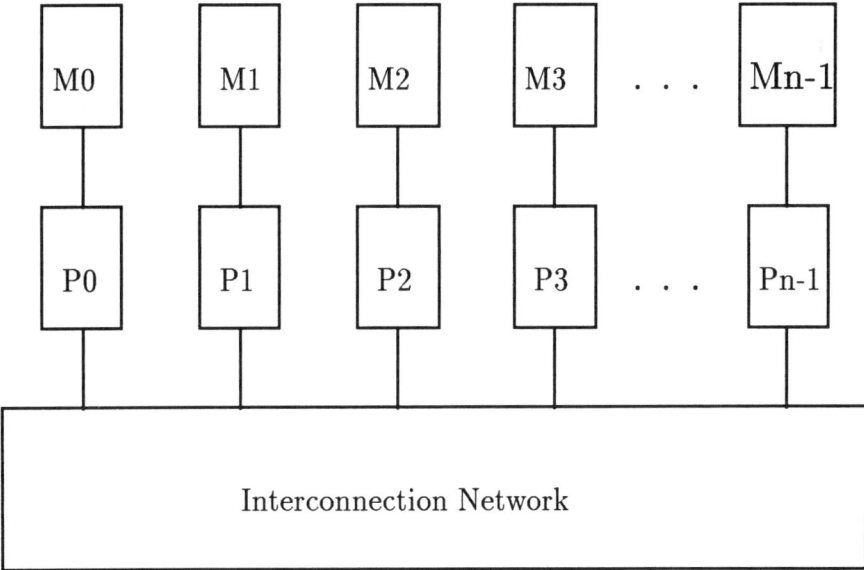

Figure 6.2: Distributed memory multiple processor system with n processors and n memories

NUMA

Non-uniform memory access describes a system that has a shared memory, but the time to access some data is less than the time to access other data. An example is a simulation of a shared memory model on a distributed memory system. The latency for fetching data that lives in a memory module attached to a specific processor will be shorter than fetching data from a memory module attached to a different processor. Memory that is faster to access could be referred to as *close memory*, while memory that is not as fast to access may be referred to as *far memory*. This inserts a new level in the memory hierarchy described in Chapter 2. NUMA machines should be equipped with caches, which should make up for the increased latency of far memory by keeping copies close to a processor in the cache. This implies that NUMA machines must provide cache coherence.

6.4 Programming Models

Multiple processor computer manufacturers provide a number of programming models that allow engineers to develop applications for those machines. A simple explanation of a *programming model* is a coupling of a description of the way the machine can be used along with a collection of tools to design applications.

There are a number of dominant programming models that are used to develop applications on multiple processor machines: the singular model, the global programming, the message passing (or local) models, and the threaded programming model. To demonstrate the difference among the different models, we can look at the implementation of a solution in each of the models for the following program fragment:

```
REAL A(1000), B(1000)

A(1) = B(1000)
DO I = 2, 1000
    A(I) = B(I-1)
ENDDO
```

This fragment represents a circular shift of the values in array B into array A.

Singular Model

In this model, a task executes on only one processor from the processor pool. If the machine uses a distributed memory model, then this is equivalent to executing that specific task on a single processor machine. If parallelism is achieved under this model, it must be task or process level concurrency, perhaps by using a process scheduler that assigns processes to specific nodes in the machine.

In this model, the circular shift example would be programmed exactly as just described.

Global Programming

In the global programming model, the user views the collection of processors as a single machine with one global memory space distributed across

6.4. Programming Models

the entire machine. Global programming languages that involve one logical thread of control are supported for programming the machine. Data objects declared in these programs are automatically distributed across the memory space of all the processors in the network, and computation is done (relatively) synchronously at all the processors. Communication between processors is implicit in the model through the layout of data objects and the distribution of computation. An example of this programming model is programming a multiple processor machine such as the Thinking Machines Corporation CM-5 using the global programming language Connection Machine Fortran, which is a language that provides many of the features of Fortran 90, with the addition of user directives that may help the compiler determine how to distribute data. The following example is written in Fortran 90.

In Fortran 90, a fragment of a global program that would perform the circular shift could use an intrinsic function to globally shift the data:

```
REAL A(1000), B(1000)

A = CSHIFT(B, DIM=1, -1)
```

Message Passing

In the **message passing** programming model, the collection of processors is viewed directly as a set of individual processing engines, each with a private memory space. Data objects are communicated explicitly through the use of functions from a message passing library. An application is programmed for this model by writing code that will execute on a single processor, with explicit communication calls embedded in the code when necessary. Intel's Paragon is programmed in this manner; a node compiler is provided for compilation of local processor code, and a message passing library is provided for communicating between processors.

In a 1000-processor machine, we can assume that each array element is allocated to a single processor. Then the circular shift can be programmed in the message passing model as a collection of programs, each of which executes on a specific processor. We may assume that a function exists to notify a process of the "name" (index) of the processor on which it executes and a function that indicates the number of processors:

```
      REAL A, B
C
C First, send my value of B to my right neighbor
C
      SEND(B, MOD(MY_ID(), NUM_PROCS()) + 1)
C
C Next, receive my left neighbor's B value into A
C
      RECEIVE(A, MOD(MY_ID(), NUM_PROCS()) - 1)
```

Threaded Programming

The threaded programming model is a hybrid of the message passing and global models. The flow of control is indicative of a global program, except that occasionally control is broken into individual threads, which are allocated to the different processors. Threaded applications are similar to global applications, except that there is much less centralized control. That is, the requirement of explicit synchronization between each statement is relaxed, and numerous threads representing different user statements may be executing in parallel.

This model is similar to the SPMD (single program multiple data) model of programming. In this model, a user writes one program that is instantiated at each node in the system. The program executes differently depending on the identification name of the executing node. Synchronization is programmed explicitly, allowing numerous threads to execute concurrently until a specific synchronization point.

6.5 Hardware Issues

The designer of a multiple processor machine must make certain decision regarding the composition of the processors, network, and memory modules, along with other peripheral processing units.

Symmetric Multiprocessing

Symmetric multiprocessors are typically made of a collection of identical processing units connected in a loosely coupled manner on a single shared

6.5. Hardware Issues

Convex C3800: New Materials

The Convex C3800 is a multiple processor machine that can be configured with up to eight processors. The processors are connected to a memory system consisting of up to 4 gigabytes and an I/O subsystem via a non-blocking crossbar network. Each processor can compute either scalar or vector operations. The memory bandwidth is 3.84 gigabytes per second. The C3800 is the first commercial supercomputer that is implemented using gallium arsenide semiconductors instead of silicon semiconductors.

---

bus (for an example, see the boxed text). These machines usually consist of more than one processor, but not more than 32 processors hooked up in a network. The granularity of parallelism is coarse: the parallel operations performed are usually at the task level. Applications are programmed using a thread model, either using a programming language that may allow for threaded operations or programming each node separately, with cooperation explicit using shared variables.

Massively Parallel Processing

A massively parallel processor computer consists of a large number of processors that execute code in parallel (thus "massively parallel"). The actual number of processors depends on the nature of the system; some systems, such as the Thinking Machines CM-2, contained up to 65,536 processors. These machines are today more commonly referred to as scalable high performance computers, since increasing the number of processors in the machine is expected to increase the computing power of the machine in a scalable fashion (see the boxed text). Because the "large" number of processors that makes up an MPP machine is disputed, defining the class of machines in terms of scalability is becoming more accepted.

The essence of MPP processing is the distribution of data and computation across the numerous nodes in the systems. The nodes are inter-

Symmetric Multiprocessing: Silicon Graphics Power Challenge

The Power Challenge supercomputer, built by Silicon Graphics, is a shared memory symmetric multiple processor system. The system can support from 2 to 18 64-bit MIPS SSR (streaming superscalar RISC) processors. Attached to each processor is a streaming 16 Kbyte cache, and the Power Challenge provides full coherent access to a 16 gigabyte interleaved memory system.

The POWERpath-2 bus provides a bandwidth of 1.2 GB/second, and may be connected to a number of high performance I/O subsystems including Silicon Graphics SCSI RAID.

The high bandwidth combined with the streaming caches provide a system that can sustain consistently high performance, instead of boasting a high peak performance!

The Connection Machine

The Connection Machine is manufactured by Thinking Machines Corporation. The current version, the CM-5, can be configured using from 32 to 16,384 processing nodes, each containing a SPARC microprocessor. As an option, each processing node may be enhanced for performance with vector units designed by Thinking Machines. The vector units (VUs) can achieve a peak performance of 128 MFLOPS/node.

The CM-5 is connected using a fat-tree for its data network. A CM-5 may be configured as a collection of a number of nodes where the number is a power of 2. The smallest configuration is 32 nodes. The largest CM-5, delivered to the Los Alamos National Laboratory, has 1024 nodes. Because of the ease of breaking up a fat-tree into noninterfering partitions, a CM-5 may be reconfigured as a collection of smaller sized machines. For example, a 256-node CM-5 may be configured as one 128-node machine, a 64-node machine, and two 32-node machines.

6.5. Hardware Issues

connected through a communications network, through which messages are sent. In most applications, both the work and the data are divided among the many processors in a machine. In the most highly parallel applications, each processor computes using its own allocated data. If processor P_0 needs a data item from processor P_1, P_1 communicates that data item through the communications network to P_0.

This style of architecture has evolved from the SIMD array processors described in the previous chapter and has traditionally been designed for applications that require significant amounts of similar computation on large amounts of mostly independent data. A simple example of this kind of application is adding two matrices and storing the result in a third matrix. The memory for each of the three matrices is distributed among the processors in the machine such that the three matrices are *aligned*. This alignment specifies that each corresponding set of elements resides in the memory of the same processor. Therefore, the matrices are divided up into "subchunks," each of which lives on one processor. Consider the following array declarations in a program to be executed on an 100-processor MPP machine:

```
REAL A(10000), B(10000), C(10000)

DO I = 1, 10000, 1
    A(I) = B(I) + C(I)
ENDDO
```

The arrays A, B and C would possibly be distributed across the MPP machine as shown in Figure 6.3.

In this example, the three arrays are distributed in mutual alignment; i.e., a specific indexed element in array A will be in the memory of the same processor that holds the corresponding indexed elements of arrays B and C. Because of this alignment, along with the assertion that all iterations of the loop may be performed in parallel, all the processors may compute on their chunks simultaneously. The time to complete the entire loop can is decreased by a factor corresponding to the number of processors in the machine. In this case, the loop executes in $\frac{10{,}000 \text{ iterations}}{100 \text{ iterations per processor}}$ of the time of a single processor, or in 1/100 the time, since 100 processors are sharing the work. This indicates a speedup of 100 over the time for a single processor. If we add more processors, the speedup will still correspond to the number of processors. For example, if the same data and computation were distributed across a 1,000-node MPP machine, the execution time

IBM's SP-1

The IBM POWERparallel System 9076 SP-1 is a collection of 8 to 64 four RS/6000 microprocessors. This machine can run a single parallel program using multiple processors, execute serial tasks on individual nodes, or perform both simultaneously. The interconnection mechanism in the SP-1 is the IBM High-Performance Switch, also known as the *Vulcan switch*. The Vulcan switch achieves a bandwidth of 50 megabytes/second. Each Vulcan chip has eight 50 megabyte/second ports in and eight out. Data that have been received at a port may wait until the destination processing unit can receive them, while other data messages may arrive and be received immediately without interference. The Vulcan switch board contains two chips, the second used as a means of "checking" the action of the first.

The Vulcan architecture maps processing nodes as points of a two-dimensional square arranged with 16 processors per vertical row. Data travels from a sending processor to the destination by going to the appropriate row, then pivoting to the right processor in that row.

This machine was developed internally at IBM through the work of its Highly Parallel Supercomputing Systems Laboratory. The SP-1 was announced only a year after the formation of the HPSSL.

6.5. Hardware Issues

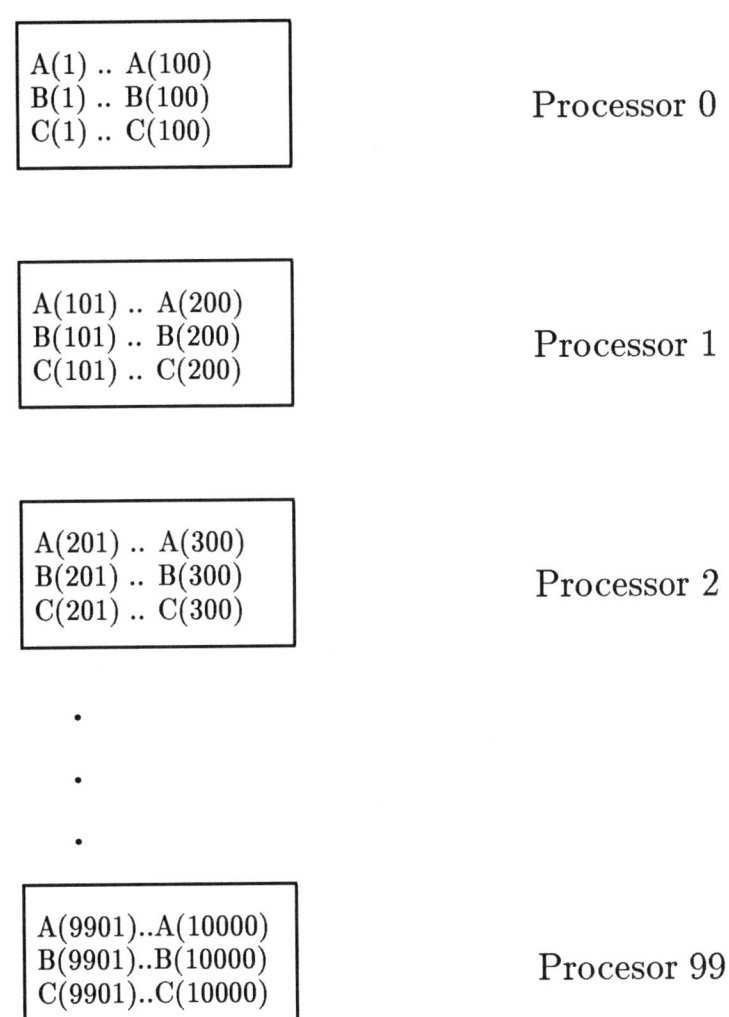

Figure 6.3: Distribution of arrays across a 100-processor MPP machine

> **Kendall Square Research: KSR-1**
>
> The Kendall Square Research KSR-1 is a hierarchical collection of rings. Each ring contains a number of proprietary processors. Attached to each processor is some memory, and the machine uses a shared memory model. When a program runs, memory pages move to the memory of the processor that requests data residing in those pages. As a memory location is referenced, the request is injected into the ring network. The request moves along the ring until a node whose memory contains a valid copy. Once the valid copy is found, the page is loaded back into the network and propagates back to the requesting node, which now also holds a valid copy of the page. When a copy of the page is written, a message is sent into the ring to indicated that the page has now been modified and that all copies are now invalid. Any requests for that page that follow the invalidation message will have to continue that invalidation message along the ring until it finds the modified copy.

would be $\frac{10{,}000 \text{ iterations}}{10 \text{ iterations per processor}}$, or 1/1000 the time. The speedup corresponds to the number of processors sharing the work. This is an example of **scalability**.

While in general, MPP applications are not as simple as matrix addition, many MPP applications are often made up of collections of matrix operations interspersed with communication operations between the different processors in the network.

Chapter 7

Collections of Workstations

As has been mentioned at other points in this book, one of the most important technical directions for high performance computing is that of networked clusters of workstations. These are referred to by many different names in the technical literature. Even though one researcher may talk of a workstation farm, another will refer to the *COW*, or collection of workstations, while another will call it a *NOW*, or network of workstations. No matter what it is called, a natural direction for the development of high performance systems is the integration of low end machinery in the model of high end systems (the boxed text has some examples).

We have already seen systems that are being built out of commodity parts. The Stanford Dash system is a good example; its processing nodes are built using Silicon Graphics clusters built with MIPS processors!

7.1 The Cluster Model

Newer models of high performance systems available from the leaders in the MPP markets are all similar in their basic architecture. The "canonical" MPP system consists of a high speed, low latency network connecting off-the-shelf processors. The distinguishing hardware factors between the canonical MPP system and the network of workstations lie in the topological aspects of the interconnection network.

High end computer manufacturers have provided systems that can provide supercomputer performance, yet the cost/performance ratio is relatively high. Not only that, but the programmability and ease of use of high end systems has traditionally been a secondary issue as opposed to performance.

MPP Systems Built with Off-the-shelf Processors

The CM-5 from Thinking Machines consists of a network of SPARC microprocessors, The Intel Paragon has a network connecting Intel's own i860 processors. The Cray T3D network connects Digital's Alpha chips. Convex's MPP machine connects Hewlett-Packard's PA-RISC processors.

In the past, the users of high end systems were willing to put up with both less ease of use and a high cost/performance to achieve the kinds of performance only available from high end systems. This notion is beginning to disappear as the performance of desktop systems improve and the network technology allows for faster interworkstation transfers. If a scalable system can be constructed completely out of off-the-shelf parts, that will reduce the two to three year time lag between the introduction of a new fast microprocessor and its integration into a high performance system.

7.2 Networks of Workstations

Many studies have been performed to determine the exact amount of actual usage of processing resources as compared to system uptime. These studies seem to indicate that, in general, workstations are idle 75 percent of the time. This would indicate that a significant amount of harvestable processor cycles can be dedicated to MPP processing!

The development of workstations farms as a viable multiple processor system relies on achieving the following goals: scalability, fast processing, fast networking, and reusability.

Scalability

One reason that the network of workstations has not been a viable high performance system paradigm is that, even though a network of workstations may perform well as a small number (say, 10) of connected systems, once the number of nodes in the system reaches a certain threshold the performance ceases to increase and may even decrease.

7.2. Networks of Workstations

The idea of scalability is that, as more workstations are added to the collection, the performance should increase accordingly. This is a major goal for the success of the workstation farm as a high performance system.

Fast Processing

Currently many processors are available that are fast enough to be used as either workstations or as nodes in a multiple processor system. When the technology for building scalable networks of workstations is available, system integrators should be able to "plug in" the latest and greatest processors. This can eliminate the multiple year lag that exists currently when integrating processors into MPP systems.

Fast Networking

One reason that cluster computing has not been successful is that the available networks connecting workstations are of low speed and low bandwidth. To have an efficient multiple processor system, the network must be able to provide much higher bandwidth at much faster speeds than is available today.

As described in earlier chapters, there is the development of the Asynchronous Transfer Mode as a network transfer mode, as well as the high speed network systems used currently in vendor-supplied MPP machines. These can be used as the first steps in providing an off-the-shelf network or switching system that is specifically designed to connect a workstation farm.

Reusability

In this sense, the term *reusability* is meant as layering the support for the multiple processor system on top of the workstation's own software system. The workstations should be usable strictly as stand-alone systems as well as pieces of the multiprogrammed environment. The use of a workstation as a node of the multiple processor system should not interfere with its use as a workstation.

7.3 Future Goals

The main goals in NOW architecture design today are these:

- *Network Processes.* Programming an application for a network of workstations should allow the abstract notion of a *network process.* This would allow the underlying operating system to coschedule processes so that interprocess communication can be performed without forcing many high cost overhead expenses. These expenses include local message buffering for unscheduled processes, protection checking, and keeping track of context throughout the entire system (nodes as well as network contents).

- *Layering on Top of Available Hardware and Operating Systems.* When a system builder can truly integrate readily available hardware and software systems into a single parallel processing system, the power of that new parallel processing system can be increased simply by "plugging in" the latest, fast processors, I/O subsystems, networks, and so forth.

- *Heterogeneous Clusters.* Today, much of the work is being done in building NOWs from sets of identical parts. In the future, NOWs will be built using different processors integrated into a single large system.

- *Parallel I/O Systems.* A parallel file system will be built out of the local file systems available at each workstation.

- *Lowering Network Costs.* The cost of sending a message from one node to another through an interconnection network is made up of the *overhead* at the processor to send the message, the *latency* of the network (i.e., the time it takes to cross the network), and the overhead at the receiving end. Extra communication library layers add to the overhead. A future goal is to build communication systems with low overhead implemented on top of low latency, high bandwidth networks.

7.4 Example

One currently available NOW is the Workstation Farm Cluster from Digital Equipment Corporation. This cluster is built as a collection of Alpha AXP workstations connected via industry standard interconnects (such as ethernet, FDDI, and soon, ATM). The Workstation Farm can be run as either

7.4. Example

individual workstations or as a parallel computer. Digital has also provided different programming paradigms for the Workstation Farm. It can be programmed using a message passing model, using standard languages (Fortran, C or C++), or as a data parallel system using Fortran 90 or High Performance Fortran.

Chapter 8

I/O

8.1 Introduction

As high performance systems get larger and faster, the needs for high performance input/output (I/O) systems become more acute. If the streaming of data into and out of a supercomputer cannot be reasonably consistent with the speed of computation, the I/O system becomes a bottleneck that can slow the entire system down.

An I/O system for a high performance computer system must provide suitable bandwidth as well as some degree of fault tolerance. The development for more efficient I/O systems has grown in two different directions: I/O servers for networks, and large (terabyte) storage systems. Examples of file server systems are NFS (Network File Service) and DFS (Distributed File Service).

For example, a scheme for building large storage systems uses many inexpensive disks, similar to those are integrated into personal computers. This system, called RAID, is described in a sequence of levels, each of which has features and characteristics that make that level suitable to certain types of computer systems.

8.2 RAID

RAID, or redundant array of inexpensive disks, systems, are collections of disk drives that are used for reliability and performance. Multiplying the number of disks used is a way of distributing the potential for the failure of a disk device over the collection of disks; this redundancy yields reliability.

Aside from fault tolerance, RAID systems provide greater bandwidth and greater capacity. In general, fault tolerance is achieved through keeping track of the parity of the data on the disks. To ensure fault tolerance, the computed parity is stored on another disk; sometimes the parity is distributed. Data is striped across disks, sometimes in a bitwise manner and sometimes in a sectionwise manner.

There are five different RAID levels:

1. *RAID Level 1.* The first RAID level consists of *mirrored disks.* All disks are duplicated, giving a set of *data disks* and a corresponding set of *check disks*. A write to a data disk is also written to a check disk.

2. *RAID Level 2.* Data stored on a second level RAID system is bit interleaved across the disks in a disk group. The parity is stored on a separate check disk. At this RAID level, there are sufficient check disks to be able to detect an error through the stored parity information and to be able to correct the error. Because only the parity information is stored on separate disks, there are fewer check disks at this level.

3. *RAID Level 3.* The difference between the second and third RAID levels is that, at the third level, there is only one check disk per disk group. Because the system can rely on the disk controllers to indicate which disk failed, less information is needed on a check disk. When a disk fails, the system checks the parities of the remaining healthy disks against the parity of the check disk, and the value of the failed bit can be inferred.

4. *RAID Level 4.* At the fourth RAID level, data units are kept in a single disk; instead of bit interleaving the data, it is section interleaved. This will allow I/O parallelism. There is still a single check disk per disk group.

5. *RAID Level 5.* At this fifth level, the bottleneck at the single check disk per group is removed, and the check information is distributed among the other disks in the group. This now allows for parallelism in both the I/O transactions and the parity updates.

8.3 Internal Parallel I/O Systems

For massively parallel processing machines, the layout of a parallel I/O system may affect the nature of the performance of the machine. An MPP

8.4. External I/O Systems

machine requires a high bandwidth, low latency I/O system. There are typically three choices for attaching a parallel I/O system to an MPP machine:

- *Attach a disk to each processing node (see Figure 8.1).* This mechanism is better suited to loosely coupled systems where an application may run separately on each node, due to the spatial locality of the processing element to the associated files. If an application is running that requires data from a disk that is not attached locally, it must make a request from the processing node that owns that data. This communication, as well as the computation interruption at the servicing node, will downgrade the system's overall performance.

- *Attach disks to the network (Figure 8.2).*

- *Incorporate dedicated I/O nodes into the network (Figure 8.3).* In this situation, files are distributed across the file system. Each I/O node is responsible for a piece of a parallel file. This mechanism will allow for configurability and scalability, because a desire for greater capacity just means adding more disks to an I/O node, or by adding more I/O nodes.

8.4 External I/O Systems

Even for supercomputers with internal I/O subsystems, there is still the issue of bringing data into and out of the the internal system. This become an issue of a high bandwidth external file service. Usually, applications that use large files may preload the files from an external file system into the internal I/O subsystem before the application is run. After the application is finished, the data stored on the internal system may then be used as input to other applications, or may be offloaded back to the external system.

> A **HiPPI** interface is a high speed network connection. HiPPI is an acronym for **High Performance Parallel Interface.**

The external system is usually connected to the supercomputer via a high bandwidth interface. One such interface is HiPPI, or high performance parallel interface. Other interfaces that may be used are Ethernet or FDDI, a fiber optic channel. The internal I/O systems are connected to the external

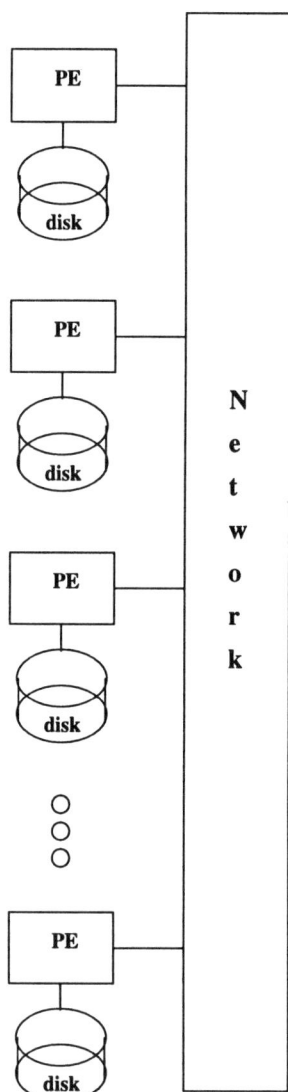

Figure 8.1: Disks attached to each node

8.4. External I/O Systems

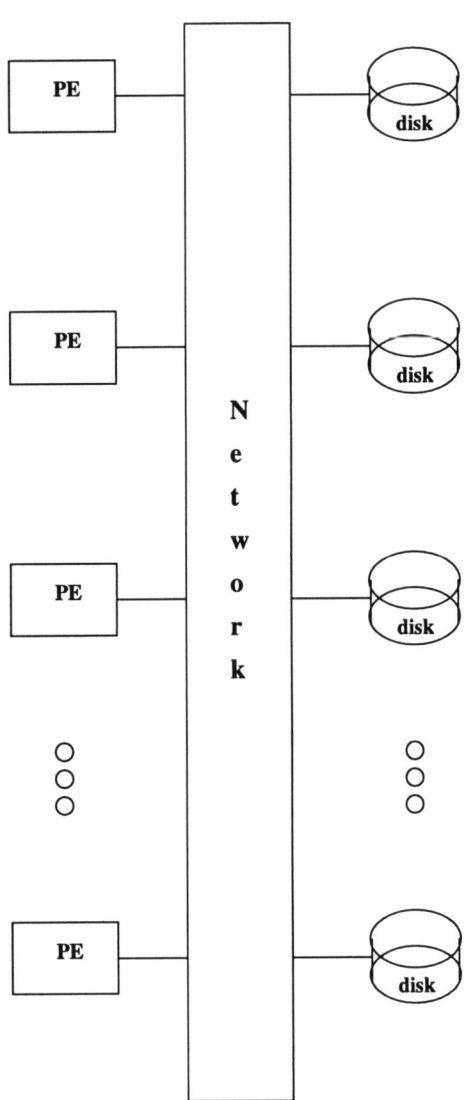

Figure 8.2: Disks attached to network

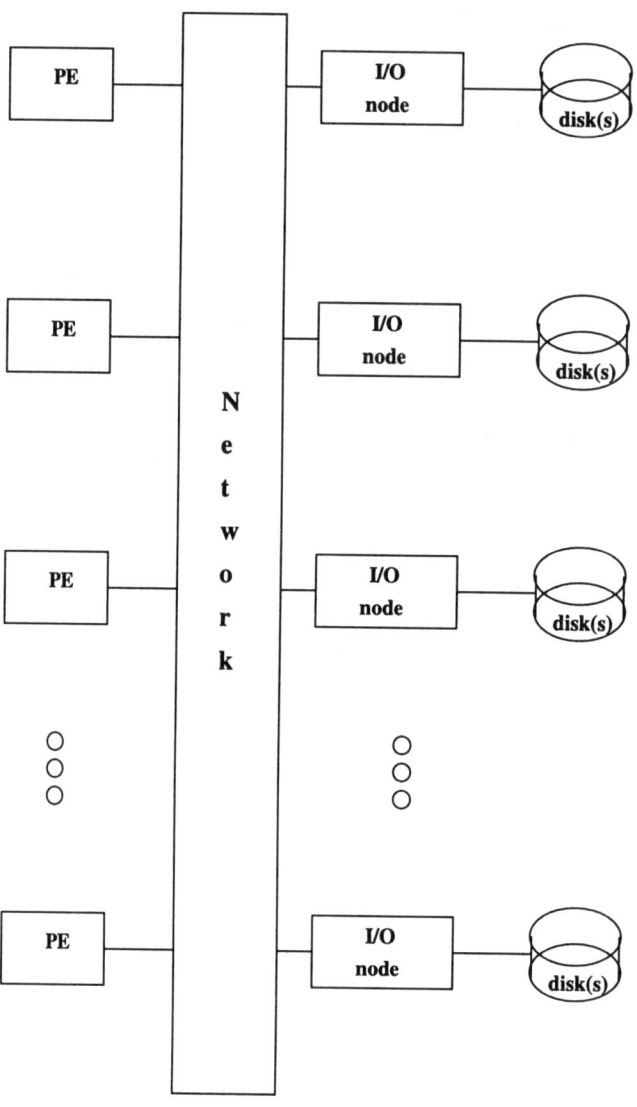

Figure 8.3: Disks attached to dedicated I/O nodes

devices through a gateway using one of the previously mentioned higher latency pathways.

Another idea is to use a solid-state storage device, or SSD. The SSD is used in the Cray X-MP and Y-MP computers, and it is used as a fast access device for files that are either preloaded or are intermediate files used by different parts of an application or different applications. SSDs are typically large sized and have relatively fast access time, which yields better performance than that of a disk.

8.5 Conclusion

The use of internal parallel file systems in many massively parallel computer systems is a recognition of the great needs for fast and reliable I/O in these large machines. As evidenced by supercomputer companies such as Intel, nCube, Thinking Machines, IBM, Cray, Kendall Square Research, and Meiko, among others, high performance I/O systems are an integral part of any supercomputer system.

Part IV

Software Issues

This part is devoted to issues regarding both programming languages and development environments for building applications for high performance computer systems.

Chapter 9

Software

No discussion of high performance computing can be complete without a section on software and applications development. Without efficient software, one could almost claim that a high performance machine is unusable.

The development of usable software for parallel machines has been a bottleneck in the progression of parallel machines into mainstream use. To facilitate the use of these machines, a number of software solutions have been proposed. These solutions include specialized languages for programming multiple processor machines, optimizing compilers that can automatically transform programs to run on high performance machines, software systems that provide message passing capability to cooperatively communicate between multiple processes, along with software systems to ensure reliability of multiprocess computations.

9.1 Languages

One design goal for a progamming language for multiple processor machines is to hide the parallelism. That is, a naive user will be able to write a program that takes advantage of the parallel hardware without needing explicit knowledge of the hardware layout. For this purpose, programming languages and programming language tools are constantly being defined and refined to provide an easy way for the user to port applications from one platform to another.

Fortran 90

Fortran is a programming language that has been around for many years, and has been a favorite language for the scientific programmer. This language is constantly being refined to make it easier for the user to program or to reflect a change in the way users look at the programming model. The Fortran standard was most recently redefined in 1990. This new standard (often referred to as *Fortran 90*) encompasses a number of features that had already been supported in many vendor-supplied compilers. A good example is the use of whole array notation instead of loop structures, allowing this program

```
PROGRAM FOO
REAL A(1000), B(1000), C(1000)

DO I = 1, 1000
   A(I) = B(I) + C(I)
ENDDO

PRINT *, A(100)
END
```

to be rewritten as

```
PROGRAM FOO
REAL A(1000), B(1000), C(1000)

A = B + C

PRINT *, A(100)
END
```

Fortran 90 is a language designed for vector and parallel computation. The short preceding code example demonstrates the use of array notation to represent whole vector assignment. Fortran 90 allows for array notation for array of all ranks as long as all the arguments are conformant.

Other features of the language that are well-suited for vector/parallel computations are these:

9.1. Languages

- *Allocatable Variables and Pointers.* Fortran 90 allows the allocation and freeing of variables (scalar or array) at runtime using the ALLOCATE and DEALLOCATE statements. Fortran 90 also allows a restricted form of pointers that was not available in the previous version of Fortran.

- *Array Section Notation.* Not only does the syntax of Fortran 90 allow for whole array assignment, it also allows for partial array assignment that is specified using *section notation*. An array section specification is written using a lower bound, and upper bound, and a stride to indicate which elements are referenced. Figure 9.1 shows an example of array section assignment:

    REAL A(21), B(7)

    B(1:7) = A(5:17:2)

    The section reference into array A specifies that all elements starting at the lower bound index 5, going until upper bound index 17, with a stride of 2. These are array elements A(5), A(7), A(9), A(11), A(13), A(15), and A(17). These elements will be stored into array B starting at index 1 and continuing until index 7. If no stride is given, the stride defaults to 1.

> The *rank* of an array is its dimensionality. A one-dimensional array is said to be of rank 1, while a three-dimensional array has rank 3. A scalar reference into one axis of a three-dimensional array results in an array section that has rank 2.

- *Enhanced Set of Intrinsics.* Included in Fortran 90 is a set of intrinsic functions that operate on array arguments. The array intrinsics fall into different categories:

    1. *Vector and Matrix Multiply Functions.* This includes DOT_PRODUCT (for dot product of two array of single dimensionality), and MATMUL (for matrix multiplication).

    2. *Array Reduction Functions.* The reduction functions all return an answer that is *reduced* in rank by one dimension. These functions

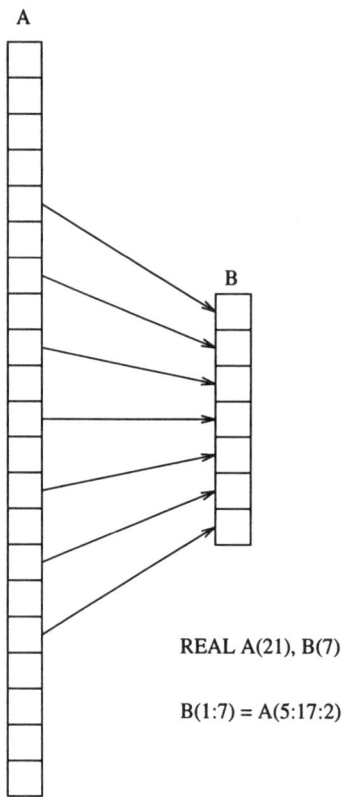

Figure 9.1: Array section assignment

9.1. Languages

include SUM (sum of array elements), PRODUCT (product of array elements), ALL (returns true if all elements are true), ANY (return true if any elements are true), COUNT (returns the number of true elements in an array), MINVAL, and MAXVAL (respectively, return the maximum and minimum values in an array).

3. *Array Inquiry Functions.* Inquiry functions are used to get information about arrays. These functions include ALLOCATED (returns true if the argument is allocated), LBOUND, UBOUND (respectively, return the lower bound and upper bound of the array argument), and SHAPE, SIZE (respectively, return the shape and size of its argument).

4. *Array Construction Functions.* The construction functions are used to build arrays out of their arguments. These functions include PACK (pack an array into a rank 1 array), UNPACK, (unpack a rank 1 array into a different array), MERGE (merges arrays under a mask), and SPREAD (which replicates an array by adding a dimension).

5. *Array Reshape Function.* The intrinsic function RESHAPE allows the user to change the shape of an array.

6. *Array Manipulation Functions.* These functions are used to move the values in an array. They include CSHIFT (circular shift of the elements), EOSHIFT (end-off shift), and TRANSPOSE (which transposes a rank 2 array).

7. *Array Location Functions.* These functions, MINLOC and MAXLOC, return, respectively, the location of the maximum or minimum value in an array.

- *The* WHERE *Statement.* Fortran 90 also allows for masked array assignment using the WHERE statement. WHERE is used to indicate a logical mask array. The mask array is used to indicate the array elements involved in the designated computation. As an example,

```
LOGICAL T(100)
REAL A(100), B(100)

...

WHERE (T) A = B
```

This statement means "for each indexed element of array T that is true, assign the corresponding indexed value of B to A."

High Performance Fortran

One of the problems with high performance computing is that there traditionally has been a struggle between the programmer and the hardware to get the best execution efficiency. The most industrious programmers will use the lowest programming level to get the best performance, recoding their important kernels in assembly language. This leads to, at best, unportable code.

While Fortran 90 gives the user more control over the way certain operations are performed (such as being able to specify vector or array operations), users may still want tighter control over the exact layout of their data on particular high performance hardware configurations. Yet, users will still want to be able to write one version of a program without having to customize it for many different hardware configurations.

The goal of the High Performance Fortran Forum (or HPFF) was to design a programming language that provides significant user control without sacrificing portability. The resulting language, called *High Performance Fortran*, is Fortran 90 enhanced with some new language features and array distribution and layout directives. Some of the more interesting features follow:

- FORALL. Even though Fortran 90 syntax allows for array expressions, certain array references are not expressible using Fortran 90 syntax. One simple example is a reference to the diagonal of a two-dimensional array. HPF syntax includes a way to express this and other array references using the FORALL statement. FORALL is used to specify array assignment in terms of array elements or groups of aray elements. Figure 9.2 shows an example of assigning the diagonal of one array into another array.

- *Library Routines.* In addition to the Fortran 90 intrinsic routines, High Performance Fortran adds extensions to the set of intrinsic routines. In particular, there are system inquiry functions. The function NUMBER_OF_PROCESSORS() returns the number of processors available to the program, or the number of processors available to the program

9.1. Languages

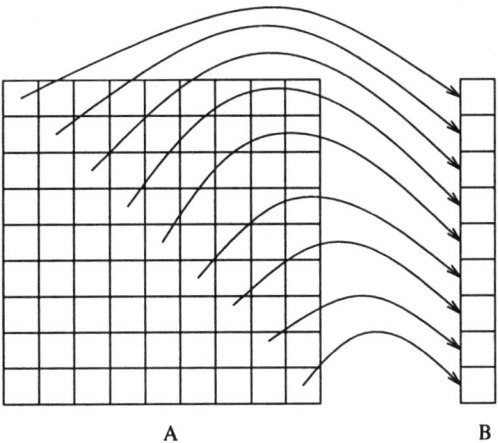

FORALL (I=1:8, J=1:8) B(I) = A(I,J)

Figure 9.2: Array assignment using FORALL

along a specified dimension. The function PROCESSOR_SHAPE() returns the shape of the implementation-dependent processor array.

- *User Directives for Data Layout.* High Performance Fortran has a set of directives that allow the user to specify different aspects of data layout. These directives range from descriptions of a processor arrangement to the way that different arrays are aligned with each other. A list of some of the data layout directives follows:

    1. HPF$ PROCESSORS. The PROCESSORS directive describes a rectilinear processor arrangement. This allows the user to describe a multidimensional processor layout across which arrays may be distributed. For example, if a user would like to view a 64 processor machine as a three-dimensional grid, the user might use this directive:

        !HPF$PROCESSORS CUBE(4,4,4)

    2. HPF$ ALIGN. The ALIGN directive is used to specify that certain data objects are to be mapped in a manner similar to certain

other objects. For example, the user may specify that two arrays are aligned with each other in an elemental manner; this means that an indexed location in the first array is mapped to the same processor as the identical indexed location in the second array:

`!HPF$ALIGN WITH B :: A`

3. `HPF$ TEMPLATE`. A template is an abstract space of indexed positions. The template is like a coordinate system onto which other items are mapped. The template itself takes up no memory space, but is used as the target for the `ALIGN` directive.

4. `HPF$ DISTRIBUTE`. The `DISTRIBUTE` directive allows the user to specify the method by which an array is distributed across a processor arrangement. Data may be distributed either in a block distribution, a cyclic distribution, or in a block-cyclic manner. The `BLOCK` distribution specifies that the data is allocated in blocks along each axis. The `CYCLIC` distribution specifies that the elements of an array are distributed along an axis in a cyclic manner by allocating each element to each processor and wrapping around again when the last processor in the processor arrangement has been reached. The `BLOCK_CYCLIC` distribution is a combination of the block and cyclic arrangements; blocks are allocated in a cyclic manner along the specified axis of a processor arrangement.

- *Global/Local Programming.* High Performance Fortran allows the programmer to take advantage of the way data is allocated to different processors by calling procedures that execute *locally* at each processor on the data that has been allocated to that processor. Data allocated to a specific processor is said to be "local" to that processor, and this programming feature, known as *global-local* programming, allows the programmer to use non-Fortran language facilities to operate on local data.

High Performance Fortran is quickly being accepted as a de facto standard for Fortran for high performance systems. One benefit of the language is its portability; an HPF program can be trivially ported to any system with a High Performance Fortran compiler. Another benefit is that despite its usefulness in building portable applications, the user directives can be used to customize an application for the hardware system on which it runs.

9.1. Languages

Many features of High Performance Fortran are being integrated into the new ANSI standard for Fortran.

C*

C* (pronounced "C-star") is a data parallel language based on the C language that was originally designed for Thinking Machine's Connection Machine. Currently, the C* language is being used as the basis for a standard definition of a C derived data parallel language.

C* is just like ANSI C except for these additions:

- *Shapes.* A C* shape is an abstract Cartesian grid that is used to define the form of parallel variables. Shapes are first class objects in C*, and shapes may be assigned to one another.

    Shapes are used to define a parallel context in which computation occurs. The following declaration in C* defines a shape that covers 100 elements.

    ```
    shape [100]S;
    ```

- *Parallel Variables.* C* allows the programmer to declare parallel variables. These variables are distributed objects allocated using a specified shape. Using the shape just defined, we can declare parallel variables:

    ```
    int p:S;
    ```

    This declares a parallel variable p to be of size 100. Parallel variables are accessed through *left-indexing*. As an example, to assign a value into the 30th element of p:

    ```
    [30]p = 1024;
    ```

- *Context.* The C* programmer can specify a context under which computation will occur. For example, consider the following program:

```
main()
{
  shape [100]S;
  int a:S, b:S;

  with (S) {
    a = b;
  }
}
```

This program indicates that the assignment of the variable b into variable a should occur using the shape S. Inside the context, the default **current shape** is S. If a function call is made within the context, the shape is passed along to the function, where it continues to be the current shape.

- *Intrinsics.* Like Fortran 90, C* also has intrinsic functions. These functions include shape intrinsics (similar to the Fortran 90 array inquiry intrinsics) and pcoord() (a function that returns a parallel integer in the current shape, where the value at each position is the index along the specified axis).

- *Communication Operations.* The use of arbitrary expressions in parallel left-indexing for parallel variable assignment may cause communication to occur. General communication in C* can be categorized as either a *send* operation or a *get* operation.

  A *send* occurs when the left-indexing expression occurs on the left-hand side of an assignment. The following example specifies that the values of src will be sent into the parallel variable dest indexed through the parallel variable index.

  ```
  shape [16]Z;

  int:S src, dest, index;

  [index]dest = src;
  ```

  A *get* operation occurs when the arbitrary index expression occurs on the right-hand side of an assignment. In this example, the values of src are "gotten" through the index parallel variable `index` into the parallel variable `dest`.

```
shape [16]Z;

int:S src, dest, index;

dest = [index]src;
```

> The C* *get* and *send* operations are just other names for our old friends *gather* and *scatter* (respectively). Gather and scatter are the indirect memory referencing operations introduced as vector memory operations on the early vector processor machines!

9.2 Compilers

It is possible to program high performance machines directly through the assembly code level for the specific machine. While this may lead to the most efficient code for a specific incarnation of a computer, many of the same applications are run on different platforms and trying to support a multitude of versions of an encoded application is a software engineering nightmare. From the engineering point of view, it is better to write the application in a portable manner, such as in a popular programming language. One problem, though, is that an application written in a high level language may not run as efficiently as an application written in a low level language.

The technology must be incorporated into the programming language tools to allow the users to take advantage of the special hardware that is built into many high performance machines. For this reason, compilers and other translation tools are developed that can automatically transform a user's program into efficient machine code. The automatic translation of a high level language program into efficient code is one of the most difficult problems for high performance system developers.

Optimizing Compilers

The first step in efficient code translation is building an optimizing compiler. The main concept of an optimizing compiler is a compiler that will eliminate as much unnecessary code (whether inserted by the programmer or inserted by the compiler) as possible, while maintaining the correctness of the compiled program. The number of **optimizations** performed by an optimizing compiler is relatively large, but here is a description of some of the more interesting optimizations:

- *Constant Folding.* Constant expressions that appear in a program may be computed at compile time, thereby eliminating the operation at runtime. As long as the compiler performs the operation in the same precision as would be computed by the target machine. For example,

   ```
         INTEGER I, J, K, L
            .
            .
            .
      10   I = 2 * (10 + 4)
            .
            .
            .
   ```

   The expression that appears on the right-hand side of the assignment statement contains only constant operands; the constant expression may be computed at compile time and replaced:

   ```
         INTEGER I, J, K, L
            .
            .
            .
      10   I = 28
            .
            .
            .
   ```

- *Expression Simplification.* When an arithmetic expression appears in a program that has an arithmeticly identical form, under most circumstances the compiler is free to replace the original expression with

9.2. Compilers

its identical form. For example, the following code fragment contains three expressions that may be simplified:

```
INTEGER I, J, K, L
     .
     .
     .
10   I = K * 1
20   J = L * 2
30   K = (I + J) * 0
     .
     .
     .
```

This code fragment may be transformed into the following:

```
INTEGER I, J, K, L
     .
     .
     .
10   I = K
20   J = L + L
30   K = 0
     .
     .
     .
```

The statement at line 10 contained a multiplication of the variable K by 1. Any integer multiplied by 1 is equivalent to itself, so the expression is replaced by just the variable K. The statement at line 20 contains the variable L multiplied by 2. In many systems, multiplication is a more expensive process than addition, so the multiplication is transformed into the less costly addition operation L + L, which is the same as multiplying L by 2. The statement at line 30 contains a multiplication of an expression by 0; since any integer multiplied by 0 is equal to 0, the entire right-hand side may be replaced by 0.

- *Common Subexpression Elimination.* Often the same expression reoccurs in a program, and the compiler can determine that the value has already been computed. For example, consider this program fragment:

```
        INTEGER I, J, K, L
        .
        .
        .
10      I = (J + K) * 2
20      L = (J + K) + I
        .
        .
        .
```

Note that the expression (J + K) appears twice in two successive statements without any intermediate modification to either J or K. The compiler can detect this and replace the fragment with the following:

```
        INTEGER I, J, K, L
        INTEGER T
        .
        .
        .
        T = (J + K)
10      I = T * 2
20      L = T + I
        .
        .
        .
```

A new variable, T, is introduced to hold the value of J + K and is used in place of both instances of the expression.

- *Copy Propagation.* When a variable is assigned a value and then the same variable appears as an operand on the right-hand side of an assignment, it sometimes makes sense to replace the variable as the operand with the expression it had been assigned earlier. One reason for doing is to exploit opportunities to perform other optimizations, such as common subexpression elimination or constant folding. Consider this fragment:

```
        INTEGER I, J, K, L
        .
```

9.2. Compilers

```
     .
     .
10   K = 15
20   J = K
30   I = (J + K) * 2
40   L = (J + K) + I
     .
     .
     .
```

After propagating the copies of J, K, and I, we have the following transformed code:

```
     INTEGER I, J, K, L
     .
     .
     .
10   K = 15
20   J = 15
30   I = (15 + 15) * 2
40   L = (15 + 15) + ((15 + 15) * 2)
     .
     .
     .
```

This can now be constant folded:

```
     INTEGER I, J, K, L
     .
     .
     .
10   K = 15
20   J = 15
30   I = 60
40   L = 90
     .
     .
     .
```

- *Useless Code Elimination.* When a statement may be determined to be *useless* (i.e., its execution has no effect, or is overridden by a later statement), the statement may be removed. Consider the following example:

    ```
            INTEGER I, J, K, L
              .
              .
              .
    10      K = 15
    20      J = 15
    30      K = J * K
              .
              .
              .
    ```

    The compiler would have copy propagated the value assigned to K at line 10 into the use of the value of K at line 30, and the value assigned to J at line 20 may be copy propagated into the use of J at line 30:

    ```
            INTEGER I, J, K, L
              .
              .
              .
    10      K = 15
    20      J = 15
    30      K = 15 * 15
              .
              .
              .
    ```

    Then, the value assigned to K at line 30 is 15 * 15, which may be constant folded:

    ```
            INTEGER I, J, K, L
              .
              .
              .
    ```

9.2. Compilers

```
10   K = 15
20   J = 15
30   K = 225
      .
      .
      .
```

The assignment to K at line 30 now overrides the assignment to K at line 10, which is now considered useless and may be removed:

```
INTEGER I, J, K, L
      .
      .
      .
20   J = 15
30   K = 225
      .
      .
      .
```

The optimizations that are provided by a traditional optimizing compiler may be sufficient for a traditional machine, but in different kinds of high performance hardware, a number of more sophisticated optimizations must be performed. Because many high performance machines are built with hardware to perform a number of operations in parallel, compilers must provide optimizations that can take advantage of the parallel hardware.

We can look at three examples of compiler optimizations that can take advantage of three different hardware paradigms. The first, automatic **vectorization**, can take advantage of machines with vector processing and fine-grain array operations. The second, automatic **parallelization**, is performed to take advantage of multiprocessing systems with a coarser granularity. The third, automatic **software pipelining**, is a mechanism for taking advantage of pipeline capabilities of RISC and superscalar processors.

Each one of these optimizations can improve the performance of "dusty deck" programs by transforming sections of old code into a format appropriate for the target hardware. We will see that there are certain constraints on the legality of some of these transformations, and those constraints will be investigated after a discussion of the transformations.

Vector Processors: Automatic Vectorization

Pipelined vector computers operate on vectors as operands to their instructions. A program written in a language that can describe vector operations in its syntax, such as Fortran 90, can be compiled into efficient code. Often, though, there are applications that have been written before the appearance of the new languages, and the users running these applications expect them to run efficiently. Therefore, the compilers for established programming languages (such as Fortran 77 and sometimes C), must be able to generate code that performs well.

Often this means that the compiler must be able to transform code portions from one paradigm to another. A good example is Fortran 77 DO loops that operate over large arrays that can also be described as specific vector operations. We can look at the example described earlier in Chapter 2:

```
REAL A(128), B(128), C(128), X
    .
    .
    .
DO I = 1, 128, 1
    A(I) = X*B(I) + C(I)
ENDDO
    .
    .
    .
```

This code fragment is an example of a Fortran 77 DO loop that performs some operations over three distinct array operands. In explicit vector form, the same fragment appear as

```
A(1:128) = X*B(1:128) + C(1:128)
```

The process by which a compiler transforms a Fortran DO loop into a vector statement is called *vectorization*. Automatic vectorization is the mechanism of recognizing operations performed on vector operands such that, when transformed, they represent an equivalent computation. It is important to note that since vector statements may modify the entire vector at once, no vector element may depend on the computed value of another vector element. This distinction is important, since some DO loops that appear to be vectorizable, are in fact not vectorizable. An example is the following loop:

9.2. Compilers

```
REAL A(128)
   .
   .
   .
DO I = 2, 127, 1
   A(I) = A(I - 1) + A(I + 1)
ENDDO
   .
   .
   .

REAL A(128)
   .
   .
   .
A(2:127) = A(1:126) + A(3:128)
   .
   .
   .
```

Even though it appears that that these two statements represent the same computation, the two programming examples represent very different operations! The semantics of Fortran say that the DO loop cascades a value written during one iteration of the loop through as the operand in the following iteration of the loop. The semantics of Fortran 90 imply that in the array statement, the values of the operands are read first and then added, and no cascading occurs. The vector statment is actually equivalent to this sequence:

```
REAL A(128), T1(128), T2(128)
   .
   .
   .
DO I = 2, 127, 1
   T1(I) = A(I - 1)
ENDDO

DO I = 1, 127, 1
   T2(I) =  A(I + 1)
```

```
       ENDDO
       DO I = 2, 127, 1
          A(I) = T1(I) + T2(I)
       ENDDO
         .
         .
         .
```

Multiprocessors: Automatic Parallelization

In a multiprocessor system, the processors and the computation may be more loosely coupled than in pipelined vector machines. Instead of transforming code into parallel vector code, a compiler might try to find parallelism on a coarser granularity. When isolated, certain chunks of a program may be carved up into separate "tasks." Each of these tasks may be assigned to different processors in a multiprocessor system. This mechanism can be referred to as *parallelization*.

In fact, parallelization is essentially identical to vectorization, after a fashion. Even thought the granularity may be different, the issues are the same: looking for computations that may be performed without exacting a potential correctness constraint when reordering the computation.

To demonstrate parallelizable code, we can look at the following sequence of Fortran DO loops (Figure 9.3 shows the code before parallelization):

```
       REAL A(128), B(128), C(128), D(128), X, Y
         .
         .
         .
100    DO I = 1, 128, 1
          A(I) = B(I)*X
       ENDDO
C
200    DO J = 1, 128, 1
          D(J) = Y + C(J)
       ENDDO
         .
         .
         .
```

9.2. Compilers

```
        REAL*4 A(128), B(128), C(128)
        REAL*4 D(128), X, Y
        ...
100     DO I = 1, 128, 1
        A(I) = B(I) * X
        ENDDO
C
200     DO J = 1,128, 1
        D(J) = Y + C(J)
        ENDDO
```

Figure 9.3: Before parallelization

The loop that begins at line 100 in the sequence operates on a scalar value X and two arrays, A and B. The second loop, which begins on the line number 200, operates on a scalar, Y, and two arrays C and D. Since the computation in the second loop does not use any of the values defined in the first loop and since the values in the first loop are not redefined by the second loop, these two loops are said to be *concurrent*. These two concurrent loops may be reordered without affecting the correctness of the program.

A parallelizing compiler might take this sequence of two DO loops and transform them into two separate tasks (see Figure 9.4). Each task may then by allocated to a different processor. If the two processors can read and write to memory in the same amount of time, the total time to complete both loops is the maximum time for either loop to finish. If the parallelized code is followed in the original program by code that cannot be parallelized, the multiple tasks must "rejoin," or *synchronize* when the tasks are complete.

Similar to automatic vectorization, sometimes the order of execution is important, and the compiler *must not* reorder *dependent* statements. There are analysis techniques for determining dependence so that the compiler will vectorize or parallelize only *independent* statements. Dependence analysis will be discussed shortly.

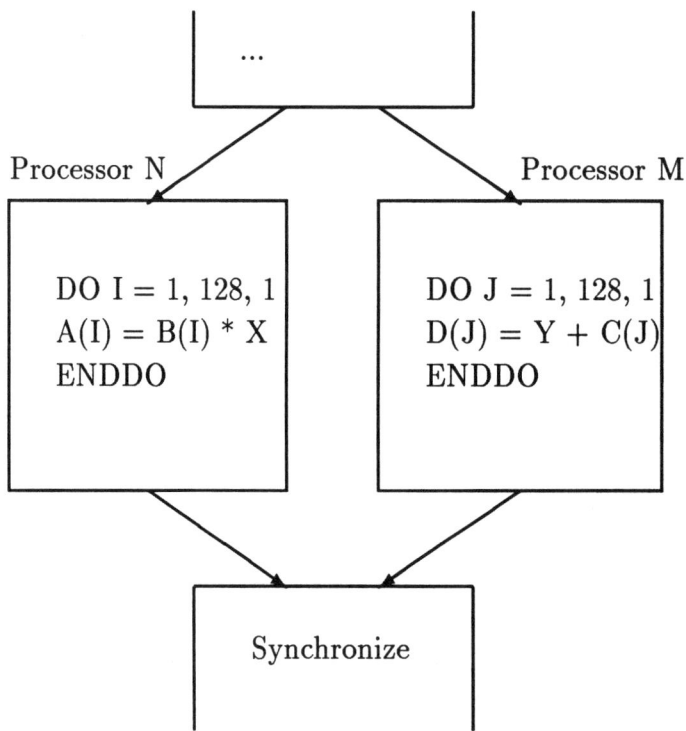

Figure 9.4: Parallelized loops allocated to processors N and M

9.2. Compilers

Microprocessors: Software Pipelining

Most new chips are designed as pipelined, multifunctional unit microprocessors. Similar in design to the original pipelined supercomputers, these micros can execute in a pipeline mode in two ways: either by pipelining the computation of values through a specific functional unit or by pipelining the computation of vector values.

Dependence Analysis

The optimizations just discussed all rely on being able to determine if any operations from a collection of operations may be performed in parallel. This determination can be made by analyzing the tasks to be performed, and checking to see if there is any reason to perform one specific task before any other. Often, a task may not be performed because it *depends* on the result of a previous task

As a way of explanation, assume that you have one job consisting of two tasks to perform, $task_A$ and $task_B$. The correctness of the entire job is related to performing $task_A$ before $task_B$, because $task_B$ uses a resource that is defined by $task_A$. We then say that $task_B$ **depends** on $task_A$. A good example is building a house, where $task_B$ is putting on the roof, and $task_A$ is building the walls: the roof cannot be put on until the walls have been built.

Instead of looking at specific tasks, we can look at program statements. The analysis to determine whether statements may be performed concurrently is called *data dependence anlysis*. More formally, one statement depends on another statement if there is a relationship between the statements based on one of these criteria:

1. **Flow Dependence.** If statement s_1 writes a value to a memory location that is read by statement s_2, then s_2 is *flow-dependent* on statement s_1.

2. **Anti-Dependence.** If statement s_1 reads a value from memory location that is later assigned by statement s_2, then s_2 is *anti-dependent* on statement s_1.

3. **Output Dependence.** If statement s_1 writes a value from memory location that is later assigned by statement s_2, then s_2 is *output-dependent* on statement s_1.

Figure 9.5: Data dependence graph for example 1

4. **Control Dependence.** A statement s_2 whose execution is dependent on the result of a conditional test performed in statement s_1 is said to be *control-dependent* on s_1.

Using data dependence analysis, we can build a data dependence graph that specifies the relationship. In this graph, vertices represent tasks, and directed edges represent dependence. A directed edge is placed from a vertex representing $task_B$ to a vertex representing $task_A$ if $task_B$ depends on $task_A$. In general, tasks that are completely independent may be executed in parallel.

Consider example 1 (Figure 9.5):

```
      REAL A(1000), B(1000)

C This is statement S1:
      A(1:1000) = 3.14159

C This is statement S2:
      B(234:496) = A(200:462)
```

9.2. Compilers

Figure 9.6: Data dependence graph for example 2

In this example, there is a flow dependence from statement $S1$ to statement $S2$, because the data read in $S2$ is written in $S1$. Because of this dependence, the execution order of the two statements is critical; reversing the order of execution will result in array B containing incorrect values. The two statements are not *concurrent* and cannot be executed in parallel.

On the other hand, in example 2 (Figure 9.6):

```
      REAL A(1000), B(1000), C(1000)

C This is statement S1:
      A(1:1000) = 3.14159

C This is statement S2:
      B(234:496) = C(200:462)
```

the statement $S2$ does not read values stored in statement $S1$, and those two statements are concurrent and may be executed in parallel.

Another example is using dependence analysis to determine vector operations. For example, consider the array addition code that we looked at earlier:

```
      REAL A(1000), B(1000), C(1000)
```

```
DO I = 1, 1000
   A(I) = B(I) + C(I)
ENDDO
```

In this example, no dependences are *carried* across the loop boundary. That is, the assignment in iteration i of the loop does not affect the execution of any other iteration. If a compiler can detect this, the loop may be directly transformed into a vector statement:

```
A(1:1000) = B(1:1000) + C(1:1000)
```

Data dependence analysis is an important part of any parallelization process, and is currently being implemented as part of most high performance compiler systems.

9.3 Operating Systems

Many multiple processor computer systems require operating system support for distributed and parallel processing. A number of operating systems have been developed to support distributed systems. As the distinction narrows between high end multiple processor systems (such as MPPs) and smaller scale multiple processor systems and workstation clusters, these distributed operating systems will be supported across the range of multiple processor systems.

> Many distributed operating systems implement a **client-server model**. In this model, a *server* is a group of cooperating processes that provide a *service* to a group of users, called *clients*.

Short descriptions of some distributed operating systems follow. Although the details of the operating systems are beyond the scope of this book, the descriptions will touch on some of the issues that are related to issues discussed earlier.

9.3. Operating Systems

Amoeba

Amoeba is an operating system originally developed at the Vrije Univeriteit in Amsterdam, The Netherlands. The goal of the Amoeba project was to build a transparent distributed operating system for a collection of computing resources such as processors, file servers, and printers. In addition, the Amoeba system was designed to build distributed and parallel applications using the programming language Orca.

Amoeba is a client-server based operating system. All services are performed on objects. An *object* is any abstract item associated with a set of operations that may be performed to it. For example, files, screen windows, and processors are all objects. For a server to perform an operation on an object, that server must hold a *capability*, or the permission, to perform that particular operation.

Amoeba also supports simple lightweight threads. Communication in Amoeba is performed either through point-to-point communication using the *Remote Procedure Call* (RPC) mechanism or with group communication operations that broadcast to all processes in a process group.

Mach

Mach is a distributed operating system developed at Carnegie-Mellon University. Mach is designed to be a transparent system that can take advantage of parallelism in the distributed system. Mach is a microkernel-based operating system used to provide a base for building other operating systems. Mach supports a large, linear virtual address space made up of fixed-size memory pages. Mach also supports shared memory objects.

Mach does not support group communication, but does provide message passing primitives. Both synchronous and asynchronous communication are supported. While the Amoeba system is designed more for a distributed system, Mach is more suited for either a single CPU system or a more tightly coupled multiple processor system.

NT

Microsoft's new operating system, NT, is designed similarly to Mach. NT supports a client-server model across many different hardware platforms.

9.4 Message Passing Systems

While the compiler can provide help in developing applications for high performance machines, often some outer system must be in place in order to provide some services, such as message passing and reliability. For loosely coupled multiple processor systems, parallelism is achieved through cooperating processes that communicate via a communications library. Communication between different processes may be either synchronous or asynchronous. *Synchronous* communication is performed when both the sender and the receiver expect to communicate at the same time. *Asynchronous* communication happens when the sender may send a message at any time without the restriction that the receiver expects the message.

A number of message passing library systems are available that allow a programmer to build an application for a message passing model. The development of MPP systems that consist of high performance microprocessors for the processing node has prompted researchers to port their message passing systems (built originally for collections of workstations) to the MPP systems. The following systems have been implemented for a slew of architectures, ranging from an ethernet-networked collection of workstations to the Intel Paragon or the Thinking Machines' CM-5.

Active Messages

An interesting system that was developed at the University of California, Berkeley, is Active Messages. This system provides a low level message passing library and interface. An *active message* is a small message that is meant to invoke a function at the receiving site. Included in the active message are the arguments to the remote call. The remote function is referred to as a *handler*. Simply, the handler function is called when the active message arrives at its destination.

Active messages provide a protocolless layer of communication on which more sophisticated customized network protocols may be built. The active messages layer may also be used as part of the library targeted by compilers for multiple processor systems.

9.4. Message Passing Systems

PVM

PVM, an acronym for Parallel Virtual Machine, is a message passing system that can be instantiated across a network of heterogeneous computers. PVM was developed at Oak Ridge National Laboratory and at Emory University as a software system that will allow a network of different kinds of Unix computers to be used as a single large parallel system.

The essence of PVM is to define a *virtual* parallel system. By combining the power of many different machines on a network, a user can treat the network as a distributed memory computer. Through PVM, users without the money to purchase large MPP machines can take advantage of distributed computing.

> A **daemon** is a special operating system process that stays resident and performs system level operations for a user when requested or carries out unnoticed system tasks.

PVM consists of two major parts: the resident daemon program and an interface library. The daemon, referred to as *pvmd*, acts as a handler for all interfacing to the message passing and task instantiation routines, through the use of sockets. The Internet UDP (User Datagram Protocol) is the socket protocol used for communication between the different nodes on the network. The interface library contains user callable functions to allow for message passing, beginning new processes, and synchronization, among others.

The programming model that fits PVM most closely is the message passing MIMD model. Because the connections between nodes on the virtual machine may be relatively slower than the network connections of a high speed MPP and because heterogeneous systems may be used to make up the virtual machine, a system running under PVM is better suited to medium- and coarse-grain parallelism. An application written for a PVM-defined virtual machine would consist of a set of processes that run as PVM tasks and communicate with each other. All tasks cooperating in an application may be part of a *process group*.

Here are some of the features available in PVM, as described in the *PVM 3 User's Guide and Reference Manual*:

1. *Process Control.* A process may become a PVM process and join a PVM process group, then later terminate its association with the process group and become a normal process again.

2. *Fault Tolerance.* PVM provides some mechanism for detection of a failure of a node that is part of a virtual machine, although the application programmer must take responsibility for making the application tolerant to the failure.

3. *Dynamic Process Groups.* The membership of a process group may change dynamically during a computation, and processes may belong to more than one process groups.

4. *Communication.* Messages can be packed and sent from one process to another, using either asynchronous blocking sends, asynchronous blocking receives, and synchronous blocking receives.

5. *Multiprocessor Integration.* PVM can integrate systems using both single node machines and nodes from multiple processor machines. For example, PVM can run on a network of workstations along with a subset of the nodes on an Intel Paragon.

Linda

Linda is another scheme that is used for cooperative communication in a distributed system. Linda, developed by David Gelernter at Yale University, allows the user to define a *tuple space*, where shared data items are posted, like a bulletin board. The tuple space is a repository for different kinds of shared data, such as shared database records or even requests for computation. The tuple space is similar to an associative memory; tuples are referred to using *keys*. When a tuple is placed in the tuple space, it is associated with a particular key. To read that tuple, it must be referred to using its associated key.

One interesting feature of the Linda system is that it is available across many different platforms. This allows applications to be built that can be run across a heterogeneous collection of hardware systems.

Linda provides a virtual shared memory, and because the system is supported by different systems, the management of the tuple space is provided transparently across heterogeneous nodes.

9.4. Message Passing Systems

Four general operations may be performed on the tuple space:

1. *out*. The *out* operation specifies that a tuple is to be published in the tuple space.

2. *in*. The *in* operation tries to match a key in the tuple space and remove it if it is found.

3. *rd*. The *rd* operation tries to match a key in the tuple space and return a copy of the found tuple.

4. *eval*. The *eval* operation creates a new tuple.

The tuple space can be used to simulate either a shared memory cooperative model or a distributed memory cooperative model. In the shared memory model, tuples are used as shared variables. Mutual exclusion can be enforced on shared reads and writes by using the *in* and *out* operations. When the *out* operation is performed, the tuple is removed from the tuple space; this prevents any other process from touching the shared item. When an update is complete, the *in* operation places the tuple back in the tuple space, effectively relinquishing the exclusive lock.

Linda may also be used to implement a distributed memory computation model, where the tuple space is used for interprocess communication. Direct interprocess communication may be implemented by using tuples created with particular keys to specify a destination process name. The only process that would receive that tuple would be the one who would know to request a tuple with a particular key.

Communications Libraries: Standardization

Because there are many different multiple processor computer systems, there is a plethora of communications libraries. Some, such as PVM or Active Messages, have been implemented on a wide range of systems, while other libraries are operational on only one hardware platform. There is now a drive to standardize a communications library that can be implemented on all systems. This standard will be called *MPI*, or Message Passing Initiative. The standard is currently under development, but should be ready within a short time frame.

9.5 Reliability in Distributed Systems

In any distributed system, a user may want to build an application to take advantage of coarse-grain parallelism. An example of a class of applications for distributed systems is a client-server system, where a set of services are shared among a collection of clients. When the data maintained by the shared servers is also shared among a number of nodes in a distributed system, the issue of making sure that all clients see a consistent view of the shared data arises.

The topic of reliability is important when running an application that uses multiple processes. Often, data is either distributed or replicated. If data is replicated, the copies of the data must be kept consistent; otherwise it is possible that a sequence of operations could result in incorrect results.

Consider a database implemented on a collection of workstations, where a copy of part of the database is replicated across a few of the nodes. If a client process makes a modification to one copy of a record while another client process is reading a different copy of that record, inconsistencies may arise. In addition, in the presence of failures of one of the nodes, it is important that information is not lost because of the failure.

For example, imagine that all savings account records are replicated at each bank in a network of banks, and an account holder is charged a $10 service charge each time a checking account balance dips below $1000. Let us assume that one person's checking account holds $1100, and that person would like to withdraw $200 from that account. To avoid the service charge, that person moves $100 from a savings account into the checking account, then withdraws the $200.

As long as the move of the $100 occurs before the withdrawal, the account holder will not be charged the service charge. But if the system arbitrarily reordered the execution of those two operations, or if the system failed *before* the move from savings, but came back up before the withdrawal, the account holder may be charged with a spurious service charge.

ISIS

ISIS is an example of a software system designed for building **fault-tolerant distributed** applications. A main goal of using a system like ISIS is the ease of building an application that allows accesses to distributed or replicated data while guaranteeing a consistent view to all clients. Similar

9.5. Reliability in Distributed Systems

to PVM, ISIS consists of a number of components: a instantiated daemon that signifies node membership in the distributed system, and a collection of application building tools that of maintaining consistency in a distributed system.

ISIS is based on the notion of causal consistency. If, in a distributed system, one event A can effect the execution of another event B, A is said to be *causally related* to B.[1] ISIS allows a user to program an application, and use ordered message passing primitives that maintain causal consistency. These order message passing primitives are referred to in ISIS as *broadcasts*, and there are different kinds of broadcasts, depending on the strength of the ordering properties needed.

ISIS was developed at Cornell University under the direction of Ken Birman and has been spun off as a separate company that now sells ISIS systems. Recently, ISIS was purchased by Stratus, Inc., the fault-tolerant hardware manufacturer.

---

[1]This is a relatively informal definition. For more formal discussion, see Lamport's article "Time, Clocks, and the Ordering of Events in a Distributed System," Communications of the ACM, vol. 21, pp. 558-564, July 1978.

Part V

High Performance Applications

There are many areas of applications for high performance computers. While an exhaustive list could take volumes to describe, the following chapters will provide a taste of the different sorts of applications being programmed. The following chapters will discuss these applications:

- Applications that model physical systems
- Seismic and oil industry applications
- Biological applications and artificial life
- Optimization problems
- Business applications
- Graphics, visualization, and virtual reality

Chapter 10

Models of Physical Systems

10.1 Introduction

The properties of physical phenomena are governed by the basic laws of physics. These laws, such as the laws of conservation of mass, conservation of energy, or conservation of momentum can be used to describe the nature of many phenomena. These phenomena can, in turn, be modeled to predict the behavior of commonplace situations, such as the motion of a baseball pitcher throwing a knuckleball, the way that gasoline and air combine and flow through an automobile's engine, or the way that air flows over an airplane's wing.

> In the context of high performance modeling, a *problem* is a description of a particular physical system about which particluar questions are to be asked and answered.

Even though the models of each of the preceding problems is different, these systems retain one thing in common: The equations describing these problems are mainly *partial differential equations*. To model a physical system and derive a solution to a particular set of questions about that model, the partial differential equations that describe the system must be solved.

In terms of high performance computing, the similarity of models is interesting because the computational methods used to solve these problems are very similar. A *solution method* is a computational mechanism for solving a problem and providing answers to questions through a controlled simulation of an event in the described system. For example, the method for solving a heat conduction problem may be the same method for solving a weather prediction problem, or it may be the same method used to solve a problem of petroleum flowing through the ground.

10.2 The Need for High Performance

The solution methods that follow have been known for many years. Why, then, is there a need for high performance computers to solve these problems? The twofold answer is simple:

- *Larger Problem Size.* The amount of computations that must be performed to solve a physical problem is relatively large, even for small problem sizes. The greater the resources available (such as more memory, CPU power, etc.), the larger is the size of problems that may be solved.

- *Fine Granularity.* Conversely, the finer the details that can be incorporated into a model, the better is the approximation to the real result. Including the finer granularity involves increasing the amount of computation that must be performed.

In addition, the nature of the problem solving process for problems described by differential equations is also compute intensive. In particular, the process of discretization and the process of domain decomposition are methods that require high performance hardware.

> The use of the supercomputer to model physical systems such as air flow, in both the airplane and the automobile industry, has led to the concept of the numerical wind tunnel. A *numerical wind tunnel* is a program implemented on a high performance machine that can be used to test the aerodynamics of some particular object design without building a physical model. This allows the designer to play "what-if?" games, integrating the numerical wind tunnel with computer-aided design tools.

In this chapter, we will examine some examples of scientific problems to be simulated and some of the mathematics used to describe the system. This will be a prolog to a description of two methods for solving the equations that are very suited to high performance computing: The finite differences method, and the finite element method. Finally, we will briefly discuss the complexity of mapping a physical model to a coordinate system.

10.3 Heat Conduction

Heat conduction is one of the mechanisms by which heat is distributed from a specific source in some enclosed area. An example of this form of heat transfer is that of a cold can of soda left sitting in a warm room. As time passes, the cold can becomes increasingly warm. The reason for this is the heat from the warm room becomes evenly distributed among all objects in the room.

In a three-dimensional coordinate system, we can measure the diffusion of heat as a function of the temperature and the conductivity of the materials through which the heat will flow. The equation used to describe heat diffusion in the absence of heat sources is Laplace's equation, and formally, this equation is

$$\frac{\partial}{\partial x}(\kappa \frac{\partial T}{\partial x}) + \frac{\partial}{\partial y}(\kappa \frac{\partial T}{\partial y}) + \frac{\partial}{\partial z}(\kappa \frac{\partial T}{\partial z}) = 0$$

where T is the temperature, κ represents the conductivity of the material, and x, y, and z are the three coordinate directions. In addition, a set of boundary conditions describes what constraints exist at the edges of system.

10.4 Fluid Flow

High performance techniques also are used to solve the equations that model flow. This section also contains descriptions of a number of different kinds of problems associated with fluid flows that are well suited for high performance computers. The methods for simulating and solving fluid flow problems can be used to model many different types of scientific and engineering processes, such as more complex heat transfer problems or problems in electromagnetics. This includes the design and modeling of airplanes, the design of efficient automobile engines, and modeling the weather. This chapter will discuss some of issues in modeling fluid flow, and then concentrate on some simple fluid mechanics problems and the methods used for solving them.

An example of a simple fluid flow problem is the flight of a completely smooth ball through an ideal, frictionless medium. As the ball moves, the air flows around the ball. As the air particles flow around the ball they move past in steady streams.

Unfortunately, real systems are not modeled as easily; air is not frictionless, and balls are not exactly smooth surfaces. This is obvious when playing golf, for example. The friction of the air with the surface of the spinning golf ball provides interactions that cause lift and drag. These can cause the ball to slice instead of fly straight to the green.

Modeling Fluid Flow

The behavior of a fluid flow is governed by the laws of mechanics (such as the conservation of mass and the conservation of momentum) and the laws of thermodynamics (such as the conservation of energy). The equations describing these laws in their full generality are extremely complex, as they describe a very broad range of fluid mechanical phenomena. Usually, simplifying assumptions are made. For example, oftentimes, viscous effects are neglected or the effect of changing fluid density may be ignored.

Incompressible Perfect Fluid Flow: The Euler Equations

Early studies concentrated on flows that are not effected by extraneous forces due to friction. This kind of fluid, referred to as a "perfect fluid," is a fluid that has no internal friction or viscosity. In the nineteenth century, Leonhard Euler formulated a system of equations describing the flow of a perfect fluid around a stationary object. We will assume that the object lives in a three-dimensional Cartesian space over the x-, y- and z-axes. We would like to determine the motion and forces as they change over time. If we assume a constant desnity (i.e., incompressible flow) then the Euler equations are

$$\frac{Du}{Dt} = -\frac{1}{\rho}\frac{\partial p}{\partial x} + f_x$$

$$\frac{Dv}{Dt} = -\frac{1}{\rho}\frac{\partial p}{\partial y} + f_y$$

$$\frac{Dw}{Dt} = -\frac{1}{\rho}\frac{\partial p}{\partial z} + f_z$$

along with a state equation relating p to u, v, and w:

$$\frac{D(\frac{p}{\rho} + \frac{1}{2}(u^2 + v^2 + w^2))}{Dt} = 0$$

10.4. Fluid Flow

where ρ is the density; p is the pressure; f_x, f_y, and f_z are, respectively, the forces in the x, y, and z directions; and u, v, and w are, respectively, the velocities in the x, y, and z directions. These equations are known as the "Euler equations."

Viscous Fluid Flows: The Navier–Stokes Equations

With a viscous fluid, there are mechanical stresses whose direction is parallel to the surface on which they act. These stresses, called "shear stresses," affect the flow of a fluid as the velocity of the fluid changes. The way that velocity and viscosity are related to the turbulence was observed and formulated by Reynolds and is now incorporated into what is called the "Reynolds number":

$$\frac{Vd}{\nu}$$

where V is some characteristic velocity, d is some characteristic length of the object, and ν is the kinetic viscosity of the fluid. As the Reynolds number increases, different kinds of turbulent effects are seen.

As the Reynolds number of the fluid increases, or when the viscosity decreases, different effects are observed. With a low Reynolds number, particles slide smoothly along the object, forming nice streams along the surface of the object. This kind of flow is called "laminar." As the Reynolds of the fluid increases, the flow along the object changes from streamlined to a sinuous flow, then tends towards random fluctuation. This kind of flow is referred to as "turbulent."

A fluid that does take into account the effects of friction is more difficult to model. In a perfect fluid, there are no shear stresses; the introduction of shear stresses complicates the relationships in the equations. The stresses in many fluids are linearly related to the derivative of the velocity. These fluids are called "Newtonian fluids." Air and water are largely Newtonian, but ketchup is, for example, is not.

The equations describing the flow of an incompressible Newtonian fluid are:

$$\frac{Du}{Dt} = -\frac{1}{\rho}\frac{\partial p}{\partial x} + \nu\left(\frac{\partial^2 u}{\partial x^2} + \frac{\partial^2 u}{\partial y^2} + \frac{\partial^2 u}{\partial z^2}\right) + \frac{1}{3}\nu\left(\frac{\partial \Theta}{\partial x}\right) + f_x$$

$$\frac{Dv}{Dt} = -\frac{1}{\rho}\frac{\partial p}{\partial y} + \nu\left(\frac{\partial^2 u}{\partial y^2} + \frac{\partial^2 u}{\partial y^2} + \frac{\partial^2 u}{\partial z^2}\right) + \frac{1}{3}\nu\left(\frac{\partial \Theta}{\partial y}\right) + f_y$$

$$\frac{Dw}{Dt} = -\frac{1}{\rho}\frac{\partial p}{\partial z} + \nu\left(\frac{\partial^2 u}{\partial z^2} + \frac{\partial^2 u}{\partial y^2} + \frac{\partial^2 u}{\partial z^2}\right) + \frac{1}{3}\nu\left(\frac{\partial \Theta}{\partial z}\right) + f_z$$

where x, y, and z are the cartesian axes; u, v, and w are, respectively, the velocities in the x, y, and z directions; ν is the viscosity of the fluid; and p is the pressure.

We define Θ as

$$\left(\frac{\partial u}{\partial x} + \frac{\partial v}{\partial y} + \frac{\partial w}{\partial z}\right)$$

These equations are often called the incompressible Navier–Stokes equations.

10.5 Methods for Solving the Equations

In the following we present two examples of methods for simulating physical systems that are described by laws expressed with differential equations.

Finite Differences

To simulate a real problem, an application builder will describe a system in terms of a model based on the laws that govern that system. These laws describe the system as a set of continuous functions over a time–space continuum. The formulation of a problem may need to express the interdependence of variables with respect to both space and time. The analyst must also decide which phenomena to incorporate into the model. For example, a heat transfer model that did not include radiation would be unwise if one were designing lightbulb filaments, but might be unneccesary for the design of an air conditioner.

Unfortunately, it is often impossible to solve a continuous model of a system due to the complexity of the equations or the boundary conditions. Instead, the analyst describes the system over a *discrete* subset of points in the time–space continuum. This involves a process of transforming the continuous laws that govern the system over the continuous set of points

10.5. Methods for Solving the Equations

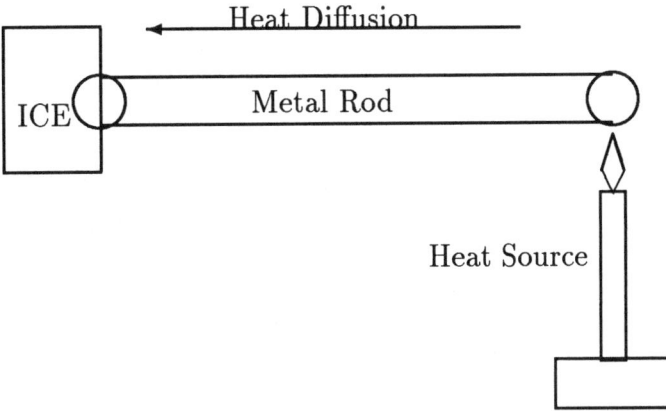

Figure 10.1: Heat conduction along a metal rod

into a system of equations over the discrete set of points approximating the behavior of the continuous equations. This process is called *discretization*.

For example, consider a metal rod that is being heated at one end (Figure 10.1). The heat will conduct in a continuous fashion along the metal rod in a direction away from the source of heat. There are laws that govern the heat conduction along the continuous space of the metal rod, but it might be simpler to divide the rod into equal-sized chunks and examine the diffusion of heat along each chunk over a sequence of time steps. Note that, because the heat travels away from the heat source, the temperature of each chunk is partially dependent on the temperature of its neighbor chunks. The process of dividing the metal rod into chunks is the process of discretization.

If the chunks are relatively big, the behavior of our discretized model may vary greatly from the actual behavior of the system. A property of a good discrete approximation is that, as the size of the chunks goes to zero, the solution of the discrete equations approaches the solution of the continuous equations.

In many systems, the state of the system changes over a sequence of time steps, and the change in state is related to the effects that happen in the spatial dimensions. One way to model this kind of system is to look at how the relations between small differences in space are affected by small differences in time. Both the temporal and the spatial differences can be

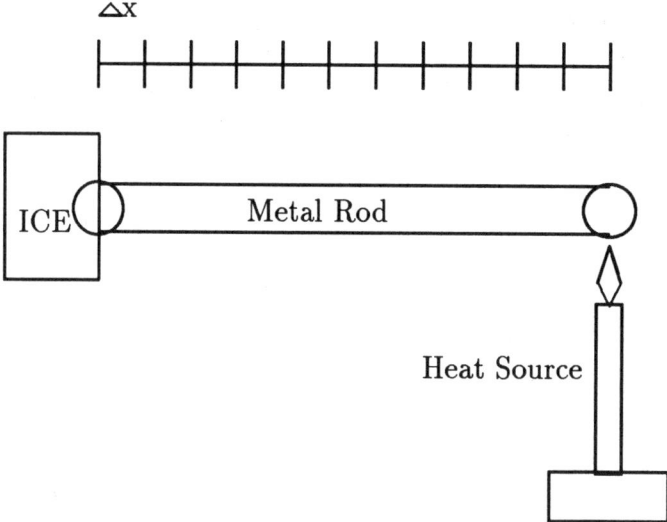

Figure 10.2: Discretized view of the metal rod

mapped to a multidimensional grid, with the values for each time step filled as during iterations of a time sequence loop. In essence, the application approximates with differences the derivatives of the physical quantities at the examined grid points. This method is referred to as *finite differencing*.

In this type of application, a multidimensional array is used to hold the differences in the spatial dimensions. In a finite difference application, each value in the grid is computed as a function of some of its grid neighbors. This incorporates how changes in a point's neighbors affect the next difference at that point.

To continue our previous example, let us look at how the temperature changes in the metal rod over time (Figure 10.2). The one-dimensional metal rod can be examined as a discrete number of points in the x-axis of a two-dimensional Cartesian coordinate system. Let the y-axis measure temperature.

In an implementation of this application, we will keep track of the changes in temperature over the different pieces of the metal rod. This can be done using a two-dimensional array. One dimension will be referenced by the piece of the metal rod, and the other will be referenced by changes in time. Into

10.5. Methods for Solving the Equations

each element of the array will be stored the temperature of the piece of metal after a specific number of time intervals. At each change in time interval, the temperature of a piece of the metal rod is a function of its temperature during the previous time interval, and the temperatures of the two pieces it neighbors. In this instance, we can use a different version of the heat equation; namely,

$$\frac{\partial T}{\partial t} = \frac{\partial}{\partial x}(\kappa \frac{\partial T}{\partial x})$$

The Finite Element Method

The finite difference method requires a discretization with a grid that is topologically rectangular. For many problems of interest, the geometry of the objects involved makes finding a grid difficult or impossible. A method of discretization that avoids this difficulty is the *finite element method*.

In the finite element method, the region is divided into a finite number of elements of simple geometric shapes. Each element represents a "piece" of the continuous space. We can examine the attributes of the system on a piece by piece method. The velocity of the fluid and the pressure on the object is determined for each of the elements using a piecewise continuous function defined for each element; the results are combined to yield an overall approximation to the solution of the original equations.

The finite element method is often used for finding the solution to sets of partial differential equations. As the granularity of the grid of finite elements becomes finer, the approximation comes closer to the true solution of the equations. High performance computers are useful, in that greater memory resources, greater computational power, and faster speed of computation allow for finer finite element grids, systems with a larger number of elements, and more accurate solutions.

In its most straightforward form, the finite element technique is a sequence of the following steps:

1. *Discretization.* The continuous space is divided into discrete regions.

2. *Evaluation of the matrices of elements.* The equations governing the system for each region are determined and configured as a set of linear equations over that region.

3. *Formulation of complete matrix of the continuum.* All the sets of linear equations are combined to form one system of linear equations that describes the entire collection of discrete regions. This system can be represented as a matrix, with each row representing a separate equation and each column representing a specific variable.

4. *Applications of boundary conditions.* The rules that govern the edges of the continuum are factored into the matrix.

5. *Solution of the system.* The system of linear equations is solved.

10.6 Problem Decomposition

When modeling large systems with high performance computers, part of the simulation involves figuring out how to divide the problem in a way that takes advantage of the high performance characteristics of the hardware. Some examples would be how to take advantage of parallel processing or how to use the distributed memory. Often, the task of decomposing a problem may also be well suited for a high performance solution. In the following we discuss two kinds of problem decomposition: data decomposition and domain decomposition.

Data Decomposition

In the finite element and finite differences methods, the region being modeled is divided into elements of simple geometric shapes, and each geometric shape is represented as a point in a multidimensional grid. Since systems may be composed of millions of these geometric shapes, the problems of decomposing the data of the model and distributing the data across processors are candidates for a high performance solution. This problem of distributing the grid points among a set of processors is referred to as the *data decomposition* or the *grid decomposition* problem.

A goal in data decomposition is partitioning the problem in a way that

- evenly distributes the computation among the grid points, and

- minimizes the interprocessor communication between grid points.

The data decomposition problem is itself a problem in *optimization*; this will be discussed in a later chapter.

Domain Decomposition

Another difficulty with modeling large systems occurs when the systems are so large that trying to accomodate all possible effects in one global simulation is extremely complex. This can be addressed by partitioning the global problem into a collection of smaller *subdomains*. Each of these subdomains is of a simpler structure, and it is easier to solve using standard techniques. This is referred to as *domain decomposition*.

Domain decomposition methods, which are used to divide a large partial differential equation problem into smaller component problems that are easier to solve, must specify the boundary conditions along the interfaces between the subdomains. These methods must also take into account the type of problem being solved. For example, when simulating three-dimensional air flow over an airplane, the domain of the airplane may be partitioned into subdomains such as the right wing, the left wing, the nose, and the tail.

10.7 Other Applications

A large collection of physical systems are described using differential equations, and consequently, many applications are implemented using the finite differences or the finite elements methods. The enumeration of applications that follows is by no means complete, but is provided to give an idea about the breadth of the industries and sciences that use high performance machines.

Structural Analysis

Many applications in structural design can be modeled using high performance machines. Among these applications are computing the stresses on different parts of a bridge to check for points needing extra reinforcement or a simulation of machine and component manufacturing processes to check for design flaws. One of the more basic structural analysis applications is crack propagation; that is, the way that the tip of a crack moves along a surface.

Imperfections may creep into a manufactured item as a result of imperfections in the process by which the item is made. Because of these flaws, different stresses are exerted in different ways, and this may lead to a fissure in the material. As the material cracks, the forces change and may cause other effects along the item's surface. If the way that a crack propagates can be modeled, then it may be easier to predict how and when a crack will appear in a material, as well as suggest a way to stop the crack from growing.

Airplane Design

Airplane wing manufacturers test the aerodynamics of airplane designs by modeling the flow of air around a representation of the plane. The most sophisticated systems attempt to model three-dimensional air flow. More modest systems may model air flow around a particular wing design in two dimensions.

Aircraft design is an example of a classical fluid flow problem applied to real design. The fluid is the air that flows around the airplane, and the applications try to model how the air flows in a way that will help lift the airplane, as well as checking how eddies form along the surface of the plane, causing turbulent affects.

Automobile Crash Analysis

Finite element codes are used to model automobile crashes. The advantages of using a computer crash simulation are great. The ability to simulate many crashes under different conditions (such as at different speeds or from different angles) can enhance the safety design of a car.

Weather

Weather forecasting through computer simulation has been a goal of meteorologists for many years. Being able to predict where catastrophic meteorological events will take place in advance can have a significant effect in the saving of lives and property.

Weather conditions change as different atmospheric variables interact. For example, some of the variables are wind velocity, air pressure, humidity, and temperature. Three-dimensional climate models are built based on the physics of fluid mechanics and convection. Equations for turbulence, thermodynamics, atmospheric pressure, and temperature are integrated into the models. Data are recorded at observation locations and collected at a central

10.7. Other Applications

Supercomputing in the Automobile Industry

Many automobile manufacturers take advantage of high performance for building better and safer cars. Here are some examples of how supercomputers are used in the automobile industry:

- Modeling the air flow around the chassis to minimize drag and reduce vibration and noise.

- Modeling the casting process to eliminate waste.

- Modeling the air and fuel mixtures flowing through the engine.

- Modeling the ignition and combustion to tune the air and fuel mixture process.

- Modeling the interaction of the tires with the air flow around the chassis.

- Simulated crash analysis and the effect on the chassis.

- Safety analysis of passengers during a crash.

All of these simulations are performed using finite difference or finite element codes.

> ### Thunderstorm Prediction: ARPS
>
> The Center for Analysis and Prediction of Storms (CAPS), located at the University of Oklahoma, is developing a computer model for predicting thunderstorms. This model, called *ARPS* (or Advanced Regional Prediction System), is the first automated storm prediction system used in tandem with the National Weather Service to perform in an operational environment.
>
> The development philosophy of the ARPS system is to build a wide-scale, general, automated model of weather prediction. The design of the system is characterized by modular code structure programmed in a scalable manner to be easily ported to any type of high performance parallel computer system, be it a MIMD, SIMD, or SPMD model. The prediction software is attached to a visualization system that allows users the ability to examine intermediate results during the simulation.
>
> ARPS was developed under the research team headed by Kelvin Droegmeier.

location, where the mathematical analysis is performed. When the analysis is complete, the resulting weather predictions are released to users of this information, such as air traffic authorities.

Weather prediction is a prime example of the type of problem discussed in this chapter. A collection of physical laws apply over a wide, continuous area. Usually, the continuous area is discretized into grid points over which a solution is sought using a computer simulation. The information regarding the initial conditions of the system is used as the input to the system, and the system is simulated for a number of time steps; the result is a prediction of the system after the simulated amount of time has elapsed.

Ocean Models

The difference in temperatures of the oceans over distinct latitudinal regions of the earth drives currents. Warm water tends to flow towards to the poles, and cold water tends to flow towards the equator. The combined effect of the earth's rotation with the oceans' convections, and the interaction with the atmosphere is another problem modeled using supercomputers.

These ocean applications, as well as atmospheric circulation applications, are generally referred to as *general circulation models*. Ocean models are used to predict the way that the ocean currents move, how water levels are affected by the currents, how tidal waves are formed, and how the currents affect local temperatures in the land areas near the currents.

10.8 Conclusion

These are just a few of the many applications using differential equations that require high performance computers. Even though the theory of finite element analysis has been available for many years, the availability of supercomputing hardware allows scientists to model physical systems of greater size and to a finer granularity than ever before.

Chapter 11

Seismic Applications

11.1 Introduction

Companies in the petroleum industry use high performance computing in different ways in their search for oil deposits. Geophysicists at oil companies are constantly trying to peer underground, looking for undiscovered oil deposits. Seismic processing has always tended to use the most powerful computers, and over time, seismologists have used computers to create ever-improving views of the underground. Today, with powerful massively parallel computers, the technology for examining collected data allows geophysicists to "see" oil deposits that were invisible to more conventional computational methods.

11.2 The Need for High Performance

The collection of geological data has been going on continuously for many years, and massive databases of seismic data have been collected. The amount of computer processing needed to transform the raw geological data into coherent views of the underlying strata is massive, and the petroleum industry has always provided good customers for high performance computers. In traditional two-dimensional seismic processing, each of the phases involves significant amounts of computation on large amounts of data. For the more complex problem of three-dimensional processing, the complexity of processing increases.

This chapter will discuss two ways that high performance computers are being used in the oil industry. One way is using supercomputers for the analysis of underground geologic structures. Another way is to model oil reservoirs to determine ways to extract oil from an oil field.

11.3 Seismic Exploration

Petroleum deposits derive from decomposed organic matter that is under significant pressure underground. The goal of geophysicists is to find locations underground that may have trapped petroleum deposits. These deposits may have formed due to different reasons. For example, as tectonic forces have shifted and moved layers of the earth, faults may have formed and aligned mineral layers in a way to form a "wall" through which underground interstitial fluids (such as water, oil, and gas) could not flow. Or, deposits may have accumulated in or around salt domes. Salt domes are geologic areas underground and underwater where ancient bodies of water had evaporated. The evaporation of this water left large salt beds that eventually hardened and moved with respect to other rocks in the same area. Because oil will not flow through salt, the existence of a salt formation may indicate possibilities for petroleum deposits.

Petroleum experts model a geologic bed by acquiring as much data about the underground structure as possible. This is done using an echo method, in which sound signals are generated and propagated through the ground. As the signals reflect against different kinds of underlying rocks, they bounce back and are recorded at the surface. This process is performed over a cross section area, and the result is a multidimensional view of the geologic structure. From the resulting image, geophysicists will look for traps, which indicate good locations to drill.

Data Acquisition

The data acquisition may be performed either on the surface of the ground or water. When it is done on the ground surface, a series of geophones is placed alongside a road, and vibratory vehicles traverse the road, using an air gun to initiate a series of signals. The geophones will then record the echoed signals. When performed on the water, a survey vessel will move along the surface of the water, initiating a series of compressed air bursts. Reflection detectors that are attached to a cable will then (in a fashion similar to the ground geophones) record the reflected signals. The collection of the reflected signals represents an image of the underground strata, much the same way that radar and sonar can be used to "see" objects.

11.4 Seismic Processing

The image must be computationally extracted from the massive amount of collected data. This involves a number of different processes. Each of the steps in seismic processing is performed to either translate sonic information into a readable form or to improve the image created. Some of the steps involve refining the data to improve the signal-to-noise ratio or removing some of the distortions that can sneak in due to unfavorable weather conditions when recording or the condition of the recording equipment. Part of the processing is done to improve the view of a single trace; other steps combine information about different traces into a combined view of the geologic structures.

11.5 Analysis of Geophysical Data

The geophysical data that is examined consists of a collection of *traces*. Each trace is of one sound wave (or "shot") through the ground recorded at one geophone. Because different kinds of rocks and minerals have different densities, sound waves travel through them at different velocities. Depth, pressure, age, temperature, and porosity affect the velocity of the sound waves as well. A shot travels down through the ground, until some of the waves reflect or "bounce" off some structure and travel back to the recording geophones (see Figure 11.1). The point that is halfway between where the shot originated (the *source*) and where the bounce was recorded (the *receiver*) is called its *midpoint*.

The traces are analyzed and then combined into *common depth point* (CDP, also referred to as *common midpoint*) gathers. A CDP represents a collection of shots with the same midpoint. For two-dimensional seismic processing, the CDP gathers are then collected and placed next to each other in what is called a *stack*. The result, which shows how sound waves traveled through different strata in the ground, is an image of the different layers. Geophysicists then review the image and, based on the kinds of structures visible in the image, can make predictions about locations underground that may hold petroleum reservoirs.

162   Chapter 11. Seismic Applications

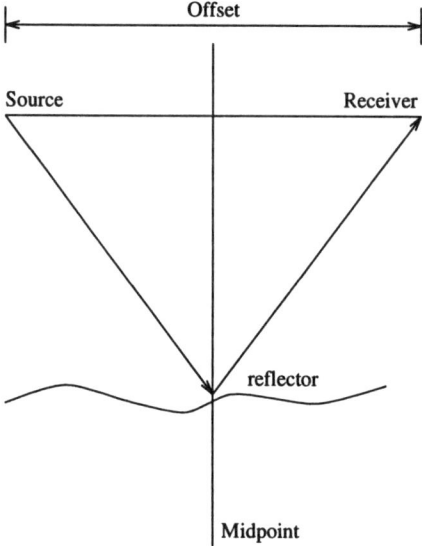

Figure 11.1: Seismic waves are "shot" from the source and received at the receiver

11.5. Analysis of Geophysical Data

Traditional two-dimensional seismic processing involves the following steps:

- Deconvolution
- Velocity analysis
- Normal moveout
- Stacking
- Migration

Each of these phases will be discussed in more detail.

Deconvolution

A standard processing technique applied to the data is *deconvolution*, which is used to remove distortion introduced when the recorded waves convolved. Signals convolve when they pass through some barrier that affects the attributes of the signal. An example of convolution is the distorted view of an oar when it is placed half in and half out of water. Deconvolution attempts to take the signal back through the distorting event in order to look at it in its purer state.

Deconvolution is performed on a trace by trace basis. This phase will undo some of the effects of prior filtering of the trace data and attempt to increase the resolution with respect to the time for the wave to travel through the ground. There may be a series of deconvolutions, with the different operations *cascaded*, one operation followed immediately by another.

Velocity Analysis

Velocity analysis is the analysis of the traces with respect to the expected velocities. Even though the log of sonic waves gives a direct measurement of their travel times, the measurement is still inexact, because a number of different types of velocities can be examined. These different velocities affect the quality of the resulting stack. Good velocity values will yield a good stack, which will in turn give the best geophysical image. This indicates that a significant amount of processing must be performed to get the best velocity information.

Determining the velocities is an iterative process. Usually, the geophysicists will have an initial velocity model of the ground being examined. Given the traveltimes of the waves, the computed velocities are matched to the model. This is then used as the base model for the next iteration, and the process is repeated until a stable model is reached.

An *offset* is the distance between the source of the seismic wave and the receiver.

The result of velocity analysis is the *coherence*, which is used to estimate the true velocity with respect to the depth. The curve of the traveltime of the seismic waves through horizontal layers is a hyperbola.

Traveltime is expressed as a function of offset. The traveltime equation is expressed as

$$t^2(x) = t^2(0) + \frac{x^2}{v^2}$$

where x is the offset, $t(x)$ is the traveltime, the time for the wave to travel from the source to the receiver, and v is the velocity. Because the offsets and the times are known, the solution to this hyperbolic function is the velocity.

Velocity analysis is used to ascertain **moveout**, which is the time difference between the traveltime of the seismic wave at some offset and the traveltime of the wave at the 0 offset. This time difference is used to adjust the velocity values as offset to the traveltime hyperbola. During velocity analysis, the data collected from the sonic recordings are used to solve the traveltime equation and then compute the differences between the solution to the equation and the actual recorded values. This is the moveout velocity.

In addition, other velocities are computed during this phase. These other velocities (including stacking velocity and migration velocity) are used to later adjust for the possibility of dips in the reflecting medium. These dips and slopes will affect the way reflections of waves interact with each other. The corrections for this will be applied during the normal moveout (NMO) phase.

11.5. Analysis of Geophysical Data

Residual Statics Corrections

When performing seismic analysis on land, there are effects of waves traveling through the near-top layer of the ground. This layer is referred to as the *weathering layer*. Waves will travel slowly through this layer. Also, the effects of this layer change with the season; during the warm weather, when swampy ground is more marshy, the waves travel slower than during the winter, when the ground tends to be frozen. This layer (also called the *low velocity layer*) affects the velocity of the waves in a number of ways, most noticeably in the absorption of seismic energy, the increased noise and scattering of the waves, and particularly in the marked change in the velocity of the wave as it passes the base of the weathering layer.

The process of correcting for the effects of the weathering layer is called *residual statics corrections*. The result of residual statics corrections provides an improvement in the quality of the CDP gathers, as well as eliminating the potential for false structures in the final image. For good results, residual statics corrections must be done before normal moveout, but it is important for the normal moveout phase to have the statics corrections performed afterwards as well. Often, these phases are repeated a number of times for the purpose of increased refinement of the data.

Normal Moveout

The normal moveout, or NMO, phase corrects the CDP gathers for differences in offset. The result of normal moveout analysis is to "straighten" the hyperbolic curves obtained by the velocity analysis phase. After NMO, a CDP gather is represented as a corrected view of how seismic waves travel down through the earth, reflected off a reflector, and travel back to the receiver. Because of the different velocities of different media, the gather shows the effects of traveling through each type of mineral or fluid. After the stacking phase, a group of gathers will show an image of the layers through which the waves have traveled.

Stacking

Stacking is the grouping of the reflected signals as detected at the different wave sensors, and averaging them to get a "better" view. The normal moveout analysis is performed on many CDP gathers, which are then grouped together, or stacked, to provide a two-dimensional view of the different strata.

If the reflectors are horizontal, the result of stacking is a relatively good image of the underground structures. If there are dips and slopes in the layers (which is most often the case), the stacked image will be incorrect due to the interaction of reflected and diffracted waves. This is corrected during the migration phase.

Migration

Dips in the underground structures will affect the image due to diffraction interference of the waves. To correct for this and, in essence, to move the reflectors to their true position in depth, the *migration* phase is performed. Migration adjusts for the fact that dips will appear shallower than they really are.

The migration phase will correct for the errors by simulating the interactions of the waves and their relationship with each other. Migration undoes the appearance of diffractions, and is done by using the wave equation and reverse propagating the real wave back to the reflector. This process is computationally intensive and is usually programmed as a finite differences simulation of the acoustic wave equation.

Once this processing is performed, a multidimensional image of the subsurface geology may be viewed. Given this view, petroleum engineers may be able to determine the different kinds of underground structures and the possibilities for petroleum reservoirs. This helps determine the effectiveness of drilling for oil or gas in particular locations.

Three-Dimensional Seismic Analysis

Three-dimensional seismic analysis is considerably more complex. To get an idea about the amount of work required, consider that even a simple three-dimensional analysis requires performing the preceding steps for two-dimensional analysis over a large number of planes across the third axis and combining the results. In fact, much more processing must be integrated into the analysis, since waves travel through three dimensions, and dips may occur across different dimensions.

> **Massively Parallel Processor Systems in Seismic Processing**
>
> Until recently, three-dimensional seismic analysis was too computationally complex to be performed on a regular basis. The amount of computational ability exceeded the available resources. But, with the availability of massively parallel processing computer systems, three-dimensional analysis is becoming a reality.
>
> The CM-5 from Thinking Machines is a popular choice for geophysicists. Oil companies that use CM-5s for seismic analysis include Aramco, Mobil, and Amoco. Western Geophysical currently uses a CM-2. The seismic processing companies CGG and Geco-Prakla also use a CM-5.
>
> Grant Tensor, a seismic processing service company, uses MPP systems from Intel to offer 3-D prestack depth migration services. Arco Oil and Gas also uses Intel supercomputers for seismic processing.

11.6 Reservoir Modeling

Reservoir simulation is a high performance computing simulation used to help in the recovery of oil from an oil field. In other words, after a significant amount of oil has been pumped from an oil deposit, the amount of pressure in the ground decreases to the point where the oil cannot be extracted. A way to increase the pressure is to inject a different fluid into the oil deposit, increase the pressure and enhance the recovery of petroleum. Enhanced reservoir recovery is an example of a problem of flow of a mixture of items through a porous medium.

Reservoir simulation is particularly well suited for high performance machines in that the problem actually involves a number of difficult issues, including the following:

- *Chemical interactions.* This includes the potential for chemical reactions between the fluids in the ground and the fluids being injected into the ground.

- *Physical interactions.*

- *Fluid flow.* This includes the description of hydrocarbons flowing through the ground, a porous medium (which may consist of rocks and dirt of different kinds and densities).

Reservoir modeling is especially difficult in that different local effects of fluid/fluid interactions and fluid/rock interactions may be difficult to incoporate into one descriptive system. In general, this modeling is done using the incompressible Navier–Stokes equations.

Another problem is that the system will change significantly as the fluid flows. For example, as a fluid like water is injected into the ground, the pressure will change, which will affect the flow of the different fluids in the ground, which will affect the velocity of the fluids, which in turn affects the pressure! Because these are values needed for the Navier–Stokes equations, the modeler must average the velocity and the pressure.

The method most often used for computing the reservoir model is the finite element model. The domain of the petroleum deposit is decomposed into finite element subdomains, the solution is found for each subdomain, and the elements solutions are combined for a global solution. This is then used as the starting point for the next iteration, and this process is repeated until the answers converge.

One additional problem has to do with how the solid material moves along with the fluids. If rocks shift in the ground, the original domain decomposition will no longer reflect the state of the system. One way to attack this issue is to use *dynamic adaptive gridding*, a method by which the grid used for the finite elements changes dynamically with respect to the simulation. By allowing the grid to change, a better simulation results.

11.7 Summary

The oil industry has always been a good customer of high performance hardware. As computational power becomes greater and the technology for analyzing seismic data advances, the ability to "see" finer views of the underground structures will improve.

Chapter 12

Biology and Artificial Life

12.1 Biology and High Performance Computing

A goal of the field of computer science is to use computers to understand more about how the human body works. Whether it is modeling functions of the body or building artifical intelligence software that tries to "think," the desire to understand human physiology has been critical in the drive to build better computers.

In this chapter, we will look at a few applications used in understanding biology. Even though these applications may have been implemented across many different hardware platforms, the implementations on high performance computers gives an opportunity to study the results on a much grander scale.

12.2 Computational Biochemistry

Many projects study the interaction of molecules within the cell. For example, the Human Genome Project is a research project to map the genes on the human chromosomes, as well as a number of other living organisms. One benefit gained from this study is the opportunity to study how different proteins are made and how these proteins interact with other molecules.

DNA and RNA are molecular polymers that carry the genetic code. Encoded in the nucleic acids are the instructions for building proteins for the maintenance of life. Supercomputer applications for computational biochemistry try to model the construction of molecules, the way that molecules take certain shapes, and how different molecules pass through membranes, as well as trying to answer different questions.

Protein Folding

One of the interesting problems in the world of computational molecular biology is the protein folding problem. Proteins are used as building blocks for many of the basic molecules used in life processes. For example, muscle tissue is built from proteins, enzymes are used to accelerate biochemical reactions, and antibodies bind with the surface of invading antigens.

Proteins consist of chains of simpler molecules called *amino acids* that fold into three-dimensional objects. The shape the protein takes is crucial to its intended use. As an example, consider an enzyme, which works by providing "docking space" for individual molecules to be bound together. The enzyme has special folds and indentations for this docking space.

Knowing the shape of a specific protein is important because it helps in learning how the job of that protein is performed. In turn, understanding the way the jobs is performed can give insight into the development of synthesized proteins to perform the same job. Members of the pharmaceutical industry are particularly interested in this problem, as it can help in the development of new drugs and treatments.

Structure

Proteins are built from chains of amino acids. The amino acid chains are useless until they bend and twist into a a three-dimensional configuration that allows the protein to attach and release other molecules. Although it is relatively simple to determine the sequence of amino acids in the chain, it is very difficult to predict how any particular chain will fold into its three dimensional form.

Amino acid residues, (or small subchains) form into two different basic motifs of structures. These structures, which are referred to as the *secondary structures*, are either spiral shapes called α-*helices* or sheets of strings of amino acids called β-*strands*. The secondary structure is a mapping of helices and strands onto a sequence of amino acids. The collection of secondary structures into a single molecule will describe the actual shape of the whole

12.2. Computational Biochemistry

protein; this form is called the protein's *tertiary structure*. Several proteins of the same type that have joined to form a single functional unit is referred to as a *quaternary structure*.

Proteins consist of a collection of amino acids connected to a *backbone*. Altough it is easy to determine the sequence of amino acids connected to the backbone, it is difficult to determine the actual shape the amino acid chain takes in crystal form. There are a small number of proteins whose shapes have actually been determined; these proteins and their structures have been entered into databases. When attempting to determine the shape of an amino acid backbone, the two problems that follow are suited to high performance computing.

Sequence Comparison

If we were to assume that each protein crystal took a unique form, it would be very difficult to predict the shape of any particular protein. On the contrary, it has been found that many proteins are grouped into families; two proteins from the same family may share certain features of a structure. The issue becomes interesting when trying to predict the secondary structure of a subchain of amino acids.

There are databases of sequences and their structures. Given a particular sequence of amino acids, the database is searched for that particular sequence. If that sequence is found in the database, then its structure may be taken directly from the database. If the sequence is not found, then the database is searched for a sequence that matches closely. The found sequence is then used as a basis for other stages of the protein modeling algorithm. The process of searching the database for closely matching sequences is called *sequence comparison*.

If sequence comparison were just a matter of string comparisons, it would be simple; instead, each entry in the database is examined to determine a measure of how closely it fits to the sequence being searched. After all database entries have been examined, the structure of the most closely matched amino acid chain is used as a starting point for predicting the structure of the amino acid chain under examination.

The size of the databases that hold the sequence-structure information is growing at a very fast pace. The larger are the databases, the more sequences there are that must be checked. This implies that more computational power is needed to perform the sequence comparison, and this can be done using

> **Dynamic Programming**
>
> The algorithm often used to perform sequence comparison is *dynamic programming*, a method used when a problem can be broken into many smaller subproblems. The dynamic programming algorithm solves the subproblems, then allows for the determination of the best solution of the global problem.

high performance parallel machines. Currently, there are implementations of the sequence comparison algorithms on the AMT Distributed Array Processor, the CM-2 and CM-5 from Thinking Machines Corporation, as well as the Intel iPSC/860.

Homology Modeling

Once the secondary structures of a protein have been found, the next step would be to predict the shape of a whole protein. Knowing that proteins are grouped into families, one may predict a general form for a particular molecule, and use a computer to refine the predicted shape until it agrees with the known electron densities. This process is called *homology modeling*. Once the structure of a protein from one family is determined, it can be used as a template for prediction of other proteins in the same family.

The shape of a protein is determined computationally by first obtaining an electron density map of the protein. There are a number of ways this information can be collected. One way is x-ray crystallography; x rays are directed at the crystal, and the waves will scatter or diffract off the electron distributions of the atoms. A photographic film is exposed to this diffraction, which manifests itself as a pattern of spots on the film. The electron density of the molecule can be computed from the patterns on the film.

The determination of the electron density map is the first step of the iterative refinement process:

1. *Obtain the electron density map.*

2. *Calculate the phase relation for the multiple dimensions.* The diffraction pattern on the film may reflect some interference between diffracted

12.2. Computational Biochemistry

rays that are out of phase. Also, because the protein is a three-dimensional object whose diffraction pattern is projected onto a two-dimensional plane, it is not always absolutely clear how the molecule relates to the diffraction.

3. *Build the model into the electron density.* The form of the folded protein is predicted and mapped in accordance with the electron density information.

4. *Refine the model.* The model is checked and refined based on molecular forces. In particular, the application program attempts to minimize the energy of the model.

5. *Check the results, and potentially reiterate.* If the resulting model is stable and its electron densities agree with the observed densities, then the model is a successful one. Otherwise, use the information from the resulting model to try again by jumping back to step 2.

The refinement in step 4 is based on forces that stabilize a chain of amino acids into a protein molecule. Among these forces are

- *Hydrophobic interactions.* This reflects the way certain amino acids interact with water molecules. A hydrophobic portion of a protein is often enclosed in the inside of a molecule, to avoid the thermodynamically unfavorable interactions with water molecules.

- *Hydrogen bonds.* Hydrogen atoms share their electrons with the atoms with which they bond. The edge of the hydrogen atom away from the bond site takes on the characteristics of a positively charged ion. This is attracted to the negatively charged parts of other structures.

- *Van der Waals forces.* These are weak attractions between molecules when they are separated by some optimum distance.

- *Electrostatic forces.* This is the effect of Coloumb's law, in which the attracting or repelling forces between ions is considered.

The access to high performance computers gives researchers the hope that difficult applications such as tertiary structure prediction will soon be implemented and working.

12.3 Neural Networks

A current topic in artificial intelligence research is simulating the way the human brain works. It is believed that if a model of the human brain can be programmed, then we can eventually build computers that can "learn" and "understand" the way that humans do.

The brain is made up of millions of cells, and information is transmitted and propagated along the neural pathways in the brain. Because of the parallel nature of neural transmissions, and the distribution of the work of neural processing, the modeling of a neural network maps naturally to a massively parallel computer architecture.

A neural network is a computer simulation of a biological process of the way a neuron works. A neural network is supposed to simulate the way that neurons work; a proper simulation is meant to provide insight into the true nature of a biological process.

It is useful to look at the makeup of a neuron:

- *The soma* is the center of the nerve cell itself.

- *Axons* are the parts of the nerve cell that produce the pulses emitted by the neuron.

- *Dendrites* receive inputs from other neurons.

- *The synapse* is the location where electrical pulses are transmitted from one neuron to another.

Configuring a Neural Network

The modeling of a biological computational process is not a new idea. The notion is to map a computation job to each of the parts of the neuron. For example, the soma itself is where a collection of inputs are combined and certain outputs are generated. This is similar to a processing element. The axons and the dendrites are the pathways that inputs and outputs travel, similar to wires. The synapses, where pulses are transmitted from one neuron to another, are similar to the connections of wires.

A neural network consists of many processing elements that are connected, either physically or logically, so that the function of neurons may be simulated. Each neuron is connected to other neurons, and associated with

12.3. Neural Networks

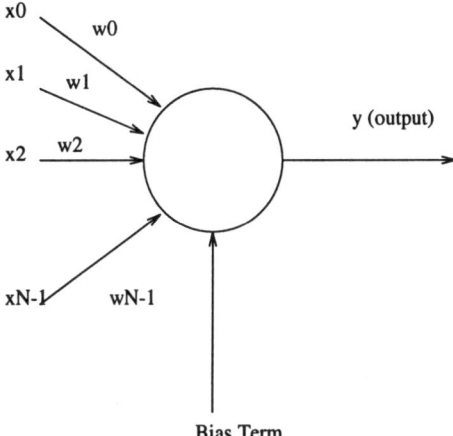

Figure 12.1: A neurode

each connection is a *synoptic weight*. Each neuron, as the computational element of the network, will compute a function of its weighted inputs, and the result is referred to as a *weighted sum*. The weighted sum is then passed as input to the neuron, which then computes a nonlinear function to produce an output value. This output value then propagates along the axon to serve as input to other neurons.

The Neurode

The basic unit of a neural network is called a *neurode* (see Figure 12.1). The neurode is the mapping of the neuron unit directly into an easily modeled computational unit.

The neurode has a series of N inputs, $x_0, x_1, ..., x_{N-1}$. Associated with each input is a weight, respectively $w_0, w_1, ..., w_{N-1}$. The weights are applied to the inputs, and the resulting values are summed. This is the weighted sum that serves as an input to the neuron.

A function is then applied to the weighted sum, adjusted using a bias value θ. The resulting value is then released along the neurons output, to be sent as input to the neurons to which it is connected.

This can be encapsulated by this equation for the output, y:

$$y = F_h(\sum_{i=0}^{N-1} w_i x_i + \theta)$$

Training a Network

The neural network may be trained. This means that the network is adaptable. We say that, when we train a neural network, that network *learns*. A network is initiated using a certain set of initial functionality. The network is configured to answer a question based on a sequence on inputs. Based on this sequence of inputs, the network is trained to learn how the initial functions correspond to known correct and incorrect answers.

There are a number ways to train a neural network:

- *Supervised training.* An external teacher oversees the training and indicates using an error signal when the network has given an incorrect answer. The error signal directly corrects the incorrect output.

- *Graded training.* An external teacher oversees the training, but gives only inexact feedback as to the correction to the error.

- *Unsupervised training.* The input translates into internal "clusters" that allows data to be filtered into categories.

- *Self-supervised training.* This is similar to supervised training, except that when an incorrect answer is given the network itself generates the error signal.

Training is a sequence of refining the weights on the inputs to the point where the network will produce an acceptable answer. It takes place as a sucessive sequence, and can be encapsulated as the following algorithm:

1. *Initialize weights.* The weights are often initialized to a value close to 0.5.

2. *Present training input.* This is the input provided, assuming some desired output goal.

12.4. Memory-Based Reasoning

3. *Calculate output.* The values are propagated along the network, using the equation described previously.

4. *Learn.* The weights are adjusted according to the degree of error. A new weight, w_i^{new} for input x_i may be computed as

$$w_i^{\text{new}} = w_i^{\text{old}} + \eta(d - y)x_i$$

where d is the desired output, and η is the gain.

New weights are determined as a factor of the previous weight values adjusted toward the ideal answer for a particular input. As the training process advances, the adjustments become smaller until the correct output is given for some particular input.

Applications

Neural networks are used for solving artificial intelligence problems, such as speech recognition, speech synthesis, and pattern recognition, among other applications.

12.4 Memory-Based Reasoning

Memory-based reasoning (MBR) is an artificial intelligence method that is used for automatic learning behavior as a function of recall from memory. A memory-based reasoning system may use the information that may be gleaned from a database of items to classify new items to be entered into the database.

MBR algorithms may be used to train an expert-system without the intervention of an expert. For example, given a database of items that have been assigned some classification, a memory-based reasoning algorithm will take a new item and search the database for items that are "similar" or "close" in some way. If a set of these items is found, the new item is assigned a classification based on the similarity to the items in the set, or the new item is assigned its own classification.

The general algorithm is

Neural Networks in Chemical Physics

An example of a set of applications that use neural networks is described in a paper by Sumpter, Guenther, Halloy, Getino, and Noid presented at the 1993 International Workshop on Artificial Neural Networks. They detail the use of neural networks for a number of chemical physics applications, such as polymer properties and dynamics; determining the relationships between coiling, temperature, number of atoms in a set of polymers measured over a period of elapsed time; and analyzing the molecular vibration and local mode energies of certain molecules.

The neural networks were first trained, and then used for predictions on much larger simulations.

The authors implemented their systems on a number of high performance systems, including

- MasPar MP-1
- Intel iPSC/860
- Intel iPSC-2
- Thinking Machines Corporation CM-5
- CRAY Y-MP
- CRAY C90
- IBM 3090
- IBM RS/6000

They found that, although currently the neural networks ran fastest on the C90, they expected scalable MPP machines to open the way for very large neural network problems.

12.5. Artificial Life

1. Find N cases nearest to the examined case.

2. Use a weighted vote to select one classification.

When an examined item falls right within a group of neighbors that have the same classification, the new item is added to that class. Otherwise, the different attributes of the items found are given a relative importance, and a weighting is calculated based on the relative importance of those attributes. The result tells the MBR system which attributes are the most important for the purpose of matching.

Memory-based reasoning techniques are used in applications for medical diagnosis, natural language prediction, document retrieval, and object recognition. In addition, MBR techniques are used in applications such as the one described previously, for protein structure prediction!

12.5 Artificial Life

Artificial life means human-made systems that exhibit attributes, characteristics, and behaviors of living organisms or systems. An example is that of the computer virus, which can infect software, then reproduce and pass itself along to other victims. Neural networks and memory-based reasoning are two applications related to artificial life; they both try to model certain life processes. As parallel computers are used for these applications, so are they used for other artificial life applications such as the following.

Cellular Automata

Cellular automata are dynamical systems consisting of arrays of units, called *cells*. These cells are initialized with some value and may communicate with their neighbors in the cell array according to some communication topology or strategy. At each time step, or *generation*, the value at each cell is reevaluated based on a function of its own value and the values of its neighbors.

Evolving Processes

Evolving processes are used to study the way that individuals as part of groups will interact with their environment. A collection of processes exists

> **Cellular Automata and Lattice Gases**
>
> Lattice gases are another type of dynamical system in which particles move along the directions in a multiple dimensional lattice. Lattice gases are used in hydrodynamic simulation to analyze flow, as well as kinetic theory, immiscible fluids, convection, and magnetohydrodynamics.
>
> Each time step in a lattice gas simulation consists of two phases: *collision* and *streaming*. During the streaming phase, particles move along the lattice. During the collision phase, the particles react with others in the lattice, potentially colliding with other moving particles. During this phase, the particles may change their local values (such as direction of motion) in a way that preserves mass and momentum.
>
> Lattice gases have been implemented on high performance machines to simulate three-dimensional Navier–Stokes flow.

within a system of environmental processes. Each process can

- Learn about its environment.
- Change its environment.
- Mutate.
- Age.
- Move.
- Calculate or reason.
- Die or kill ("terminate").

An evolving processes system can be used to model different laws of biological systems of individuals that act collectively (such as population growth). These systems are inherently parallel, and are nicely suited to parallel computer systems.

Genetic Algorithms

Genetic algorithms are algorithms where the searching and computational techniques embedded in the algorithm are allowed to develop based on random variation and selection. A *genotype* in a genetic algorithm may be represented in some discrete form (usually a string of characters) defined by some fixed expression rules.

At each generation (a sequence of time steps), the algorithms may change as a result of these operations:

- *Reproduction.* Individual strings are copied according to a fitness value that is based on a function of how well the represented algorithm performed. This fitness function determines how certain strings will contribute to the next generation, similar to natural selection.

- *Crossover.* A crossover occurs when strings exchange information at a randomly chosen site. This exchange of information often allows the propagation of "notions" related to specific tasks between different "strains" of algorithms.

- *Mutation* Mutation is the occasional random replacement of characters in a particular string. It is often used as a protection against unwanted loss of information, such as when a crossover changes the nature of the way an algorithm may work.

Genetic algorithms have been used for image processing, pattern recognition, optimization problems, and medical imaging, as well as the basis for investigating the evolution of pictures and textures in computer animation.

12.6 Conclusion

Between practical applications for molecular biochemistry and applications in artificial life and artificial intelligence, high performance computer systems are being utilized more efficiently and effectively. As the software applications become more mature, the ability to learn more about biological systems through the use of supercomputers will enable researchers to learn more about how humans live and think.

Chapter 13

Business Applications

13.1 Introduction

The constant flow of data and information in the business world has beaten a path for the inroads of high performance computing. A number of applications are well suited to utilizing supercomputing resources:

- *Large database applications.* The proliferation of computer systems over the last 20 years, in both mainframe and workstation models, has allowed huge databases to be collected. The amount of data available has surpassed the ability of mainstream computation systems to process that data. In some instances, queries on databases with millions of records may take days or even weeks to complete.

- *Financial instrument pricing.* Although some types of financial instruments have well-formed procedures for determining their values, there are exotic and interesting instruments that can be priced only by using a probabilistic method that performs an analysis of multiple simulations.

Each of these cases is an example of applications that can be sped up through the use of a high performance computer system. The following sections will describe these applications and show how the application may be sped up.

13.2 Large Database Applications

With the constant accumulation of data, many databases have grown in size to the point where they are almost unmanageable by conventional computers. Companies with huge databases are turning now to MPP systems for their transaction processing, data query, and decision support needs.

> Transactions in a database system include adding records, deleting records, and updating records. A *query* into a database is a request for a collection of records that share certain attributes. For example, a query might ask for all records of employees that have worked for the company for four or more years and are between the ages of 18 and 34.

Client-server database systems are made up of two types of processes: the server, which maintains the data, and the clients, who make requests for information from the server. With MPP machines, the work of the server application is allocated to the different processors and disk drives. One way that parallelism is used in database systems is breaking queries up into small components and running each component on a different processor. As more queries are broken up, more processors are put to work. A complementary use of parallelism is the distribution of database tables across the many processors. This enables the database software to perform parallel database operations.

Although the use of supercomputers can increase the speed of transactions and queries, what makes the use of high performance computers interesting are new ways to use more traditional applications (such as *decision support*).

13.3 Decision Support

Decision support is a term to describe the use of querying large databases to answer specific marketing questions as quickly as possible. In some cases, even using high speed mainframe computers, a moderately simple query might require a week to 10 days to complete. This excessive turnaround time can cause a significant bottleneck when decision processes rely on the result of one of these queries, yet this was the problem encountered by American Express.

The American Express Corporation has amassed a massive database of card members. To process a query into the card member database, the

13.3. Decision Support

Hardware for Transaction Processing

Tandem, one of the pioneers in parallel processing for nonscientific commercial applications, provides both hardware and software systems for relational database management and decision support. Tandem's Himalaya line of massively parallel servers run on-line transaction processing software called NonStop Transaction Services/MP and NonStop Transaction Manager/MP.

Sequent's Symmetry 2000/750, a symmetric multiprocessing system that uses Intel 80486 microprocessors, runs database management applications using Oracle software.

Oracle also has been ported to IBM's SP-2. IBM also plans to port its DB2/6000 relational database software to exploit the parallelism of the SP-2.

NCR provides both symmetric multiprocessor and massively parallel systems for client-server transaction processing and decision support.

Parallel Relational Databases

Many companies that provide relational database management, database querying, and transaction processing systems are now shifting towards parallel processing. Currently, the Oracle Corporation has announced the availability of a parallel Oracle that runs on multiple processor machines. Sybase has announced the availability of NonStop SQL/MP, a massively parallel relational database. Informix provides a product called INFORMIX-OnLine Dynamic Server, which makes use of a multithreaded parallel processing database architecture, designed for single processors, networks of workstations, symmetric multiprocessors, and massively parallel machines.

current database program, SELEX, can take up to 10 days before providing a result. If management and marketing decisions are to be made based on the result of queries into this database, then an 8 day response time for a query is too long.

An American Express subsidiary, Epsilon Data Management Inc., convinced the parent company to purchase two CM-5 systems from Thinking Machines Corporation. Epsilon wanted to provide a system to utilize the massively parallel processing power of the CM-5 to perform a number of interesting tasks. The resulting project, called *Quantum*, is soon to replace SELEX as the decision support system at American Express.

One goal of this venture is to reduce the database query response time. A query that once took eight days would be expected to complete in two to three hours instead. By being able to ask more questions in a shorter amount of time, American Express will be able to refine its queries and get better results.

13.4 Data Mining and Micromarketing

Once the information in massive database has been accumulated, the owners of the database would like to make the best use of the information. One way to do this is gather records from the database that exhibit similar attributes. Searching through massive databases looking for small groups of similar records in one method of *data mining*. Data mining is used for a number of purposes, one of which is *micromarketing*. Some uses of data mining for micromarketing are

- *Specialized mailings.* A mail-order company might want to target a very select group of customers, who exhibit a certain buying pattern, for a specific catalog mailing. By limiting the mailing to customers who have a history of purchasing certain kinds of products, specialty catalogs can be mailed only to those customers likely to respond, resulting in a saving of mailing costs.

- *Customized mailings.* Similarly, a mail order company might want to build a customized catalog for certain customers that is targeted to their purchasing behavior.

- *Checking for attrition.* A credit card holder is said to "attrit" when canceling the card membership. Data mining can be used to build a

13.5. Intelligent Business Software

profile of customers who have atritted, and then periodically search through the database for customers who match this profile. Being able to prevent attrition is a very important business goal for credit card companies.

The use of high performance computers for decision support and data mining applications can significantly improve the turnaround time for queries, giving businesses greater leverage in making important decisions.

13.5 Intelligent Business Software

Decision support is one application that uses massive database systems to help solve business problems. Decision support applications usually operate as questions once a pattern has been defined, looking for others that match that pattern. A new collection of tools is being built, dubbed *intelligent business software* systems, that are used rather to "find the pattern," given the people.

Intelligent business software systems are designed to make use of neural network and genetic algorithm techniques implemented on a high performance system to do intelligent business prediction.

Darwin

Thinking Machines Corporation has developed a suite of intelligent business applications for the CM-5. This suite, called *Darwin*, consists of four separate tools:

- *StarMatch*, which uses memory-based reasoning to compare a single database record to all other records in parallel to seek out similarities for the sake of predicition.

- *StarNet*, which is a parallel neural network tool used for developing predicition models on large datasets.

- *StarTree*, which is a parallel implementation of CART, or Classification and Regression Trees, a technique for breaking data into subgroups looking for prediction rules.

- *StarGene*, which is a tool that uses genetic algorithms to improve prediction techniques.

13.6 Example in Parallelization: Options Pricing

Another application that may take advantage of parallel hardware is option pricing. Derivatives pricing is discussed here; portfolio management is covered in a later chapter.

An option is a commonly available financial instrument used to transfer risk from one type of investment to another. In the world of exchange-traded options, there are typically two kinds of options: calls and puts. An option is the right to buy or sell another security at some specified *strike* price some time in the future. A *call* option is the right to buy the security; a *put* is the right to sell that security. For simplicity, the discussion will be limited to call options.

As an example, assume a stock's current price is $100. An options *writer* (i.e., a person who makes a market in options for that stock) may buy or sell a call option that has a strike price of $105 and an expiration date that is 90 days in the future. Options are sold as a set of options to buy 100 shares of the underlying stock.

A speculator who expects the stock's price to rise way above the option strike price within the time to expiration would buy the option. If, at the end of 90 days, the stock's price is $110, the option buyer may *exercise* the option and buy the stock at $105, then sell it at the market rate of $110 and make a $5 profit per share.

Conversely, a speculator who expects the price of the stock to decrease may sell a call option for some amount of money. If the price of the stock goes down to $98, the option expires worthless, because no one would buy the stock at $110 when it is sold on the market at $98. The bearish speculator make a profit on the cost of the sold option.

A person who sells an option on a stock limits the profitability of an increase in the value of that stock to the difference between the current price and the strike price of the option. That is, if a person who owns the stock sells the $105 strike-price call just described, the owner limits the potential profit to the difference between the current price and $105. If the price of the stock goes above the strike price, that extra profit goes to the option buyer. This is an example of how options are used to transfer risk.

13.6. Example in Parallelization: Options Pricing

The Value of an Option

Simply, a person who buys an option either expects some movement in the underlying security's price or has noted that the option is mispriced. An option is mispriced when the rate of return of buying the option and selling some amount of the underlying security is greater than the current riskless rate of interest. Usually, if an option is noticed to be mispriced, an arbitrage expert may make some transactions to take advantage of the mispricing and thus drive the price back to its correct price. Because of this, it is important to be able to correctly determine the price of an option.

At any point in time, an option's value depends on a number of parameters:

1. *Current price*, the price of the underlying security at the time of pricing.

2. *Strike price*, the price at which the security will be transacted in the future.

3. *Riskless rate of interest*, the interest rate that is guaranteed.

4. *Expected payout*, the expectation of the value of buying the underlying security.

5. *Time to expiration*, the number of days until the expiration date of the option.

6. *Volatility*, a gauge of the inclination of the movement of the underlying security. In other words, it is a value used to describe the standard distribution of the price of the security.

Closed Formulas

Given these parameters, traditional options may be priced using one of a number of methods. A closed (that is, nonexpansive) formula for pricing options was developed by Fisher Black and Myron Scholes that takes into account the preceding parameters. The Black–Scholes method for pricing options is the standard used to price regular call and put options.

The Stochastic Path Model

A number of types of options do not fit into a closed formula model. The reason for this is that the payoff of the option depends on the path that the price of the underlying security takes over the lifetime of the option contract. Not surprisingly, one type of these options forms a class called *path-dependent* options.

For example, one kind of option is called an *Inside Trading* option. This option can be exercised only if the value of the underlying security remains within a specific price range during the contract period. Another option type is the *Down-and-Out* option, which has no payoff if the price of the underlying security falls below a specific value before expiration of the option. These kinds of options cannot be priced using traditional closed formulas. Instead, a model developed by Mark Hull Dobson of the Metals Derivatives group at Barclay's Bank called the *stochastic path model* can be used.

The stochastic path model for options pricing is an example of a stochastic, or random, process. A stochastic process is a random function of time that is characterized by a probability density function.[1] The particular implementation described here uses a modified Brownian motion model, which investigates variance between the current price of an item to the future price of an item.

There are no closed formulas for path-dependent options; the *only* way to price path-dependent options is to simulate the paths through which the price of the underlying security can move over the time period covered by the contract period. Given a large number of simulated paths, the resulting collection of prices can be collected and analyzed. As long as the prices fall within a normal distribution, the simulations will provide a reliable estimate of the security price.

The stochastic path model assumes that, although the price of a security moves in an unpredictable way, the price does not move in a completely random way. If the price of a security is $100 today, there is a greater probability that tomorrow the price will be $99 than $1. In other words, the price movement of the underlying security depends on a function that has a deterministic portion and a random portion. We call that the *stochastic function*.

Each *path* consists of a sequence of prices. At each interval, that interval's price is derived from the previous interval's price by applying the stochastic

---

[1] As defined by Charles Doering in *1990 Lectures in Complex Systems*, p. 6.

13.6. Example in Parallelization: Options Pricing

function to the previous interval's price. A collection of paths (typically 5000 to 10,000) must be created to have a valid sampling for the statistical analysis.

Implementation

The stochastic function consists of two terms, the deterministic term and the random term. The deterministic term is based on the expected return of the underlying security over the time to expiration. The random portion of the function is based on numbers drawn from a set of normally distributed numbers between −1 and 1. These numbers are then combined with the volatility and applied to a price to affect a price difference in each interval in each path.

The simple implementation of the stochastic path model is easily described in Figure 13.1.

Parallelization

The code in Figure 13.1 represents the functionality of a multiple path simulator. The number of paths is specified by the variable **simulations**. In that implementation, all paths are simulated in a sequential order. In fact, this stochastic path model is an example of an *embarrassingly parallel* algorithm. Because all the paths are independent, no constraint forces a specific evaluation or computation order.

Because there is no order constraint on the execution of the paths, we can parallelize the execution of the complete simulation on a multiple processor computer. This is done by distributing the paths among the collection of processors. For example, given a multiple processor machine with 16 processors and assuming we simulate 8192 paths, we can distribute 512 paths to each processor. Even though we can parallelize the computation of all the paths, we cannot parallelize the computation of each interval along any specific path, because the value of a price along a path at any time interval depends on the value of that price from the immediately previous interval.

We can take advantage of computer languages such as High Performance Fortran to implement the same simulation. High Performance Fortran, which uses the array features of the Fortran 90 standard, can allow a programmer to specify parallel computations using array syntax. We can specify the

```c
double max(a, b) { return((a > b) ? a : b);}
double option_price(underlying, K, simulations,
      interest_rate, payout, time_to_expiration,
      volatility, intervals)
    double    underlying;          /* spot price of the underlying security */
    double    K;                   /* Strike Price */
    int       simulations;         /* number of simulation paths */
    double    interest_rate;       /* riskless rate of interest */
    double    payout;              /* payout of underlying */
    double    time_to_expiration;  /* time to option expiration */
    double    volatility;          /* volatility of underlying */
    int       intervals;           /* periods in each path */
{
    int       i,j;                 /* counters */
    double    probability;         /* probability of each path */
    double    price;
    double    delta_t;
    double    first, second;
    double    path_price;
    double    z;
    probability = 1.0/(double)simulations;
    price = 0.0;
    time_to_expiration = time_to_expiration/365;
    delta_t = (1.0/(double)intervals) * time_to_expiration;
    first = ((interest_rate - payout -
        (0.5*(volatility*volatility))) *
        delta_t);
    second = (volatility * sqrt(delta_t));
    for (i=0; i;simulations; i++) {
        path_price = underlying;
        for (j = 0; j ; intervals; j++) {
            z = number_from_random_dist(-1.0, 1.0);
            path_price = path_price * exp(first + (second * z));
        }
        price = price + (max(path_price- K, 0.0) * probability);
    }
    /* calculate the present value of the price */
    price = exp(-interest_rate * time_to_expiration) * price;
    return(option_price);

}
```

Figure 13.1: Single processor C code for options pricing

parallel nature of the stochastic path model in the following HPF function, described in Figure 13.2.

In this implementation, the paths are distributed among the available processors. An array PATH_PRICE is used to signify the paths. In order to indicate how many processors are available, HPF provides a function called NUMBER_OF_PROCESSORS() that, at runtime, will return the number of processors in the multiprocessor system. We create a virtual processor map, called ALL_PROCS, to describe a one-dimensional array of processors.

In this function, the number of paths (denoted by the parameter SIMULATIONS), defines the size of the array PATH_PRICE; this is the array into which all the paths will be computed. PATH_PRICE is distributed across the processors using the HPF directive DISTRIBUTE. The number of paths that we allocate to each processor is the total number of paths divided by the number of processors. This is indicated by the HPF$DISTRIBUTE directive BLOCK(SIMULATIONS/NUMBER_OF_PROCESSOR()).

Even though we distribute the paths among all the processors, the amount of work performed over the number of intervals is the same at each processor. It is a good idea, then, to keep the information we need for computing each subsequent interval at all the processors. This is done by distributing the data used to compute each interval at all the processors. The array Z is used to hold the values from the random distribution over the interval (-1.0, 1.0). This array is a two-dimensional array: the first dimension is the same size as the number of paths, and the second dimension is the same size as the number of intervals. The asterisk in the second dimension of the DISTRIBUTE directive for Z is used to indicate that the second dimension is to be completely allocated at each processor.

The inner loop represents an array computation over the entire collection of paths. In essence, the program computes each interval over *all* the paths at the same time. At the end of the loop, all paths have been computed and the result can be accumulated by multiplying all the paths by the probability of that path occurring (part of the stochastic process) and then adding those values together. The rest of the function is the same as the previous sequential C version.

13.7 Conclusion

Sophisticated business applications are rapidly joining the mainstream. As high performance systems become more mature and reliable, we will see

```fortran
      DOUBLEPRECISION FUNCTION OPTION_PRICE(UNDERLYING, K, PAYOUT,
     & VOLATILITY, INTEREST_RATE, TIME_TO_EXPIRATION,
     & INTERVALS, SIMULATIONS)

      INTEGER SIMULATIONS
      INTEGER I,J
      DOUBLEPRECISION K
      DOUBLEPRECISION UNDERLYING
      DOUBLEPRECISION INTEREST_RATE
      DOUBLEPRECISION PAYOUT
      DOUBLEPRECISION TIME_TO_EXPIRATION
      DOUBLEPRECISION VOLATILITY

      INTEGER INTERVALS

      DOUBLEPRECISION PROBABILITY, PI, TWOPI

      DOUBLEPRECISION A_PRICE
      DOUBLEPRECISION DELTA_T, LOCAL_TIME_TO_EXP
      DOUBLEPRECISION FIRST, SECOND

      DOUBLEPRECISION PATH_PRICE(SIMULATIONS)
      DOUBLEPRECISION Z(SIMULATIONS, INTERVALS)
!HPF$PROCESSORS ALL_PROCS(NUMBER_OF_PROCESSORS())

!HPF$DISTRIBUTE Z(BLOCK(SIMULATIONS/NUMBER_OF_PROCESSORS()), *) &
!HPF$ ONTO ALL_PROCS

!HPF$DISTRIBUTE PATH_PRICE(BLOCK(SIMULATIONS/NUMBER_OF_PROCESSORS())) &
!HPF$ ONTO ALL_PROCS

      INTEGER TIMEOFDAY(2)

      PI = 3.14159D0

      PROBABILITY = 1.0D0/SIMULATIONS
      PRICE = 0.0D0

      LOCAL_TIME_TO_EXP = TIME_TO_EXPIRATION/365
      DELTA_T = (1.0D0/INTERVALS) * LOCAL_TIME_TO_EXP

      FIRST = ((INTEREST_RATE - PAYOUT - (0.5*(VOLATILITY*VOLATILITY)))
     & * DELTA_T)

      SECOND = (VOLATILITY * SQRT(DELTA_T))

      CALL FILL_WITH_NUMBERS_FROM_RANDOM_DIST(Z, -1.0, 1.0)

      TWOPI = 2*PI

      PATH_PRICE = UNDERLYING
      DO I = 1, INTERVALS

          PATH_PRICE = PATH_PRICE *EXP(FIRST + (SECOND * Z(:,I)))

      ENDDO

      A_PRICE = SUM(MAX(PATH_PRICE-K, 0.0D0) * PROBABILITY)
C /* CALCULATE THE PRESENT VALUE OF THE PRICE */

      A_PRICE = EXP(-INTEREST_RATE*LOCAL_TIME_TO_EXP)*A_PRICE

      OPTION_PRICE = A_PRICE
      RETURN
      END
```

Figure 13.2: Data parallel HPF code for options pricing

13.7. Conclusion

Distribution of Data Using Directives

The way that data is allocated across a grid of processors in a multiple processor system is important for achieving good parallel performance. A general goal is to avoid communication of data from the memory of one processor to the memory of another. As described earlier, the programmer can lay out the data using *directives* that give hints to the compiler on how to ultimately distribute the data.

In the case of the stochastic path model, almost all of the computation can be done without communication of data! The reason is that most of the computation at a single processing node is done on a series of paths that have been allocated to that same processing node. The data for the values from the random distribution that are to be used for that node's path computations are distributed to that node, so no communication is needed to get those data.

The only communication in this function occurs after the interval loop, at the call to the Fortran intrinsic function SUM. The summation occurs over the entire array of paths, which is distributed across all the processors, and so the partial sums of each processing node's paths must be combined with the partial sums from every other processing node's paths. These partial sums must be communicated among the processors or collected at one specific control processor.

more examples of their use in the business world. As indicated by American Express's use of the CM-5 for its decision support system, more and more important companies are welcoming high performance hardware into the business world.

Chapter 14

Optimization

14.1 Introduction

A class of problems, referred to as *optimization problems*, are typically formed as questions of the optimal allocation of limited resources. Optimization problems can range from relatively simple questions to extremely complex questions. On the simple end are questions about the allocation of funds to assorted departments in a company or the most nutritious menus for school lunches. On the complex end are questions such as the least costly allocation of airline crews to airline routes or optimal investment selections in portfolio management.

14.2 The Need for High Performance

Even though there are a number of methods for minimizing optimization problems, certain optimization problems are considered to be "hard," and the desire to solve these problems drives the use of high performance computers. For example, some problems can be solved when they are of a small enough size, but as the size of the problem grows, greater computation resources, such as memory or computing power, are required. When the optimum of a problem of a certain size is found, the trend would be to increase the size of the problem and find the optimum for that larger problem.

> The *size* of a problem is not an exactly defined term, but often depends on the number of variables, as well as the amount of storage space used for the solution matrices.

> **The Traveling Salesman: Part 1**
>
> A classic example of a combinatorial optimization problem is the traveling salesman problem. A salesman is assigned to peddle his wares in a number of different cities across the country. A certain cost is associated with traveling from any one city to any other city, either in airfare, train fare, or gasoline. He must visit each of the cities exactly once, but he may visit those cities in any order. At the end of his visits, he must return to his home city.
>
> Associated with any particular roundtrip is the total cost of moving between each city in the sequence. He is responsible for his own travel expenses, and so it is in his best interest to visit the cities in an order that leads to the least costly roundtrip.

Also, because the formulation of an optimization problem will affect the method chosen to solve it, certain new problems may not have a good algorithm available yet. Often the methods chosen to solve these problems may involve heuristic algorithms that try to limit the number of possible solutions to investigate when searching for an optimum. These problems also benefit from the use of supercomputers.

This chapter will contain a brief description of optimization problems, and we will look at a solution method for linear programming, the *simplex method*. This will be followed by specific examples of complex optimization problems whose optimal solutions are found using supercomputer technology. The first example is that of optimal airline crew scheduling, which involves allocating airplane crews to specific flights out of a set of scheduled flights. The second example discussed is that of optimization techniques used to properly price a portfolio of financial objects whose price depends on a number of different variables.

14.3 Formalization

Problems in this class often will conform to a question of finding the minimum of a set of variables based on some set of static inputs and subject to a collection of *constraints*.

An optimization problem can be characterized as a problem of mini-

14.3. Formalization

mizing a function over a set of variables that are constrained by a set of constraints. Formally, a nonlinear constraint problem poses the problem, find a set of variables $x_1, x_2, ..., x_n$ in a vector $\mathbf{x}$ such that a function $F(\mathbf{x})$ is minimized. Associated with this problem is a set of constraints

$$q_j(\mathbf{x}) \leq 0, 1 \leq j \leq M$$

and a set of bounds,

$$x_i^L \leq x_i \leq x_i^U, 1 \leq i \leq N$$

Example: The Diet Problem

A good example of a simple optimization problem is the diet problem. Given a collection of n different foods, each of which has some concentration of m nutrients and some fixed cost, and given some minimum daily requirement of nutrients to be consumed, what foods should be bought such that the minimum daily requirement of nutrients be met at the lowest cost?

Let x^j be the number of ounces of each food j, $j = 1 \cdots n$.

Let b_i be the minimum number of milligrams required of nutrient i, $i = 1 \cdots m$.

Let c_j be the cost per ounce of food j.

Let a_{ij} be the number of milligrams of the ith nutrient in one ounce of the jth food.

The resulting formulation of the problem is to minimize over the foods $(x^1, \cdots, x^n)$ using the cost function

$$c_1 x^1 + \cdots + c_n x^n$$

under the constraints:

$$a_{11} x^1 + \cdots + a_{1n} x^n \geq b_1$$

$$\vdots$$

$$a_{m1} x^1 + \cdots + a_{mn} x^n \geq b_m$$

and $x^j \geq 0$ for $j = 1, \cdots, n$

Categories of Optimization Problems

Optimization problems may fall within a smaller category. Some of the categories include

- *Unconstrained problems.* There are no constraints in the problem.

- *Least-squares problems.* The function to be minimized is related to the sum over the squares of another function applied to the variables.

- *Linearly constrained problems.* The constraints are of the form

$$Ax(\geq, =)b$$

and

$$l \leq x \leq u$$

- *Bound-constrained problems.* The variables are bound by upper and lower bounds, such as

$$l \leq x \leq u$$

- *Linear programming problems.* The function to be minimized is a linear function.

- *Quadratic programming problems.* The function to be minimized is a quadratic function.

14.3. Formalization

The Minimum Cost Flow Problem

Given a network consisting of a set N of nodes $(n_1, n_2, \cdots, n_k)$, and a set A directed arcs of the form (i, j) (indicating the direction is from node n_i to n_j), if we let

- a_{ij} be the cost of the arc (i, j)
- b_{ij} be the lower flow bound of the arc (i, j)
- c_{ij} be the upper flow bound of the arc (i, j)
- x_{ij} be a flow value from node i to node j

then the minimum cost flow problem is to find a set of flows x_{ij}, minimizing

$$\sum_{(i,j) \in A} a_{ij} x_{ij}$$

such that the flow values x_{ij} are within the bounds

$$b_{ij} \leq x_{ij} \leq c_{ij}$$

The sum of the flows entering all nodes must equal the sum of the flows exiting all nodes. This, known as a *flow conservation constraint*, is formulated as

$$\sum_{j|i,j \in A} x_{ij} - \sum j|j, i \in A x_{ji} = s_i$$

where s_i is called the *supply* of node i.

Flow arcs may have a positive or negative cost value. An arc with a negative cost value indicates that flow moves in the opposite direction.

A *flow vector* $\mathbf{x}$ (consisting of all the x_{ij}s) is a *feasible* solution to the minimum cost flow problem if none of the problem constraints is violated. A minimum cost flow in this network would be the least expensive method for moving objects ("flow") through the network. A particular instance of such a problem is said to be feasible if there exists at least one feasible solution.

> **The Traveling Salesman: Part 2**
>
> There is currently no known polynomial time algorithm for computing the solution to the traveling salesman problem. This problem is one of a set of problems referred to as *NP-complete* problems; *NP* stands for "nondeterministic polynomial." This means that, although there is no known polynomial time algorithm for finding a solution, any correct solution can be *verified* in polynomial time with respect to the size of the input.
>
> This implies that, to find the optimal path for the salesman, *all* paths must be examined. The number of possible paths is *exponential* with respect to the number of cities that need to be visited.
>
> Despite the large number of possible paths, the difficulty of the problem is not as bad as one might think. One strategy is to look at subproblems consisting of a subset of the cities and optimize for that subset, and then combine the subproblem solutions. The issue then becomes whether the local optima are global optima also or if any two subproblem solutions are connected by a monotonic path.

This problem is an example of a *linear programming* problem. It is similar to the matrix computations we saw earlier in regard to the solution of simultaneous equations. As long as the constraints remain static (e.g., the cost of any particular food does not change from day to day), this problem is easily solvable using standard techniques such as the simplex method, developed by George Dantzig in 1947 for solving linear programming problems.

As the number of variable increases or as the number of constraints increases, solving linear programming problems requires more computing power.

14.4 The Simplex Method

The primary goal of most methods for finding the optimal solution of any problem instance is *cost improvement*. Cost improvement may be achieved by "guessing" a possible optimal solution, then iteratively improving that solution by modifying it slightly to generate a different feasible solution at a lower cost. If we use the minimum cost flow (MCF) problem as our canonical

14.4. The Simplex Method

optimization example, then given a feasible solution, a lower cost solution may be found if flow may be pushed through a cycle in the graph that has a negative cost. One method for identifying negative cost cycles is called the *simplex* method.

The simplex method is an iterative method that uses an alternative representation of the graph to generate negative cost cycles. This representation, called a *spanning tree*, is a subgraph of the original graph that is a tree and includes all the same nodes as in the original graph. Associated with each arc in the spanning tree is a cost. As described in [7], each iteration (also called a *pivot*) of the simplex method does the following:

1. *Pricing.* Modify the tree by inserting an arc to create a negative cost cycle. This new arc is called an *in-arc*.

2. *Ratio test.* Push the flow through the cycle without violating any of the feasibility constraint of the network. As the flow is pushed through the cycle, the result is that at some point the flow entering a node may hit its specified upper or lower bound.

3. *Update.* The arc through which the flow hit its bound is called the *out-arc*. This arc is removed from the created cycle, which results in a different feasible spanning tree, potentially with a lower cost.

A number of questions need to be asked at different steps of each iteration. For example, how does the algorithm choose an in-arc, or how do we ensure that the algorithm continues to improve the cost of the feasible solutions? In addition, the number of possible distinct feasible solutions is finite, so the algorithm should eventually terminate. But there may be many different ways for the algorithm to generate solutions, and it is possible for the method to examine the same solution many times.

Parallel Implementation of the Simplex Method

The three steps just outlined may be implemented in parallel, as described in [6], on a global shared-memory multiprocessor computer. Once the spanning tree (also called the *basis*) is formed, all arcs fall into one of two sets: the *basic* arcs (in the basis), and the *nonbasic* arcs (not in the basis). The pricing step chooses an in-arc from the nonbasic arcs, and the third step updates the basis, reducing the costs and also swapping basic and nonbasic arcs.

A parallel implementation would want the pricing and update steps to be performed simultaneously. Unfortunately, there are dependencies that might prevent this. Two possibilities are

1. Trying to perform both steps at the same time. It is probable that the algorithm will not choose an unupdated value. If it does, the algorithm may stall until the needed value has been updated.

2. Decomposing the steps into smaller substeps, and performing each of the substeps in parallel.

Each substep becomes a task, and a mutual exclusion scheme is used to keep the tasks scheduled correctly. As a task is created, it is added to a global task queue. All nodes execute a protocol in parallel that checks the task queue, potentially pulling a task off the queue and performing it. Priority is given to certain tasks to minimize the time between pivots. In many tested problems, this method achieved linear (or better) speedup.

14.5 Airline Crew Pairing

One example of an optimization application that is currently being solved using high performance computers is the Airline Crew Pairing problem. A *crew pairing* is a sequence of flights that begin at a crew's home base, visits a number of cities over a selected time period, and then returns to the crew's home base. The selected time period typically ranges from two to three days.

There are a number of important issues that affect the optimal crew pairing. First of all, legal regulations affect the amount of time that a crew may spend flying during a specific duty period, as well as total duty time. Also, the labor rules that guarantee minimum pay for a crew, regardless of the time spent flying, introduce a number of additional cost components. One of these costs is incurred if a crew must spend a long time overnight between flights; another is incurred if the crew must be ferried back to the home base (i.e., *deadheading*).

Other considerations also must be taken into account. Crews are trained for a specific type of aircraft. A pilot trained to fly an Boeing 767 will not be asked to fly an Airbus 320. Usually, each plane type would be considered as a separate problem.

There is a preference for keeping a crew on the same plane as long as possible. On the other hand, the hub-and-spoke network system allows for

14.5. Airline Crew Pairing

crews to change planes at a hub, and this may lead to a better pairing. The crew pairing problem is a combinatorial problem, and the minimization of the cost of an optimized crew pairing can prove a substantial savings to an airline.

Finding a Solution

Typically, the different formulations of the crew pairing problem can be formulated based on different constraints:

- *The daily crew pairing.* This is the day to day crew pairing problem.

- *Crew-base constraints.* Once a solution to the daily problem is found, it must conform within the distribution of crews among the different home bases.

- *Weekly scheduling.* This is the coordination of the daily schedules into a weekly schedule.

Traditionally, combinatorial problems such as the airline crew pairing problem have been solved as a sequence of *subproblem solutions*. A subproblem is a piece of the original problem that is handled separately.

To solve the global problem, first a set of workable solutions to the subproblems are found, and those solutions are used to find as optimal a solution as possible for the whole problem. In our example, the process of subproblem selection would consist of using a feasible solution and grabbing a small collection of covered segments from that feasible solution. This collection of segments is much smaller than the set of all segments and is considered to be a subproblem.

The crew pairing is then performed for the smaller subset of segments. If a better (i.e., more cost-effective) solution can be found for that subset, that more optimal subproblem solution is checked for correctness back in the original global solution. If the new subproblem solution does not introduce any conflicts in the global solution, that covering set replaces the original subset of segments. By incrementally optimizing over pieces of the large problem, the solution tends towards optimality for the global problem.

Integer Programming vs. Linear Programming

The airline crew pairing problem is a problem of finding an exact match of crews to segments, and each segment is covered only once. If the problem is formulated as a two-dimensional matrix, with the columns representing all the possible pairings and the rows representing each segment, then a matrix element contains the value 1 if the pairing is in the solution, and 0 otherwise. Because any solution to this problem must have all integer values (in this case, 0 or 1), it is an example of an *integer programming* problem. While linear programming problems may be solved using the simplex method, integer programming problems are much more difficult to solve, and the simplex method is insufficient.

One way of using methods such as the simplex method for integer programming problems is to relax some of the constraints. For example, in the airline crew pairing problem, a relaxation would be to allow variables with values that fall between 0 and 1. The resulting problem is a linear programming problem, for which an optimal solution may be found using methods like the simplex method. In reality, a nonintegral solution does not really make sense; a fractional value would indicate that a segment is *partially* covered by one crew pairing and partially covered by another. But the solutions that are found in the linear programming version can then be used to find near-to-optimal solutions to the original integer programming problem. This can be done by using the solution to the continuous problem to "fix" certain variables (at either 0 or 1). Fixing these variables may simplify finding the optimal solution to the integer programming problem or may show that with a certain variable fixed there is no feasible solution. If no feasible solution exists under those circumstances, then that eliminates a number of possible solutions from examination. By continuing to prune out unfeasible solutions, a feasible optimal solution may be found.

14.6 Portfolio Management

As described in an earlier chapter, the pricing of simple financial instruments (such as options) can be performed using high performance machines. Many financial institutions create complex portfolios that contain a collection of financial instruments that are related in some manner. The value of the portfolio must then be calculated. An example of such a portfolio is a collection of mortgaged-backed securities. A mortgage-backed security is a pool

14.6. Portfolio Management

of mortgages from which an interest is sold to investors. The investors then receive a share of the mortgage cash flows. A mortgaged-backed security is an example of an *interest rate contingent* cash flow.

The valuation of a mortgage-backed security is difficult because these securities have features of both bonds and options. They are similar to bonds in that the investor "lends" money and is rewarded with an interest payment on the original investment. They are similar to options in that the borrower has the right to prepay the entire loan at any point during the loan repayment period. This prepayment will preclude any future interest payments, thereby introducing the risk of an option. Also, because loan values fluctuate based on the current rate of interest, not only does a change in the current rate is a factor in the valuation of the security, but the possible interest rates in the future over the lifetime of the portfolio (usually 30 years) need to be factored into the value.

Because interest rates are viewed as changing on a month-by-month basis, there are 360 time intervals over which the interest rate will change, as well as 360 different possible states at the end of the term. Because interest rates can move up or down at each time interval, there are 2^{360} possible paths through which interest rates can move. The cash flows of the portfolio depend on using simulations of the paths through which interest rates move and analyzing the value of each security in the portfolio through each path. After a large number of paths have been simulated, the results are combined and the price is adjusted for the time value of money.

Analyzing Securities

Considering the number of possible paths that interest rates may take, it may be very time consuming to analyze one security. When building a portfolio, many different securities must be analyzed to choose a set that, when combined into one portfolio, has a maximized rate of return with a minimized degree of risk.

Portfolio management is an example of a *multiobjective* optimization problem. In this problem, there are two objectives: maximizing return while minimizing risk. The frontier of the risk vs. return plot indicates the best choices (i.e., best return for the lowest risk) for a portfolio. In Figure 14.1, the security represented by X has a very low risk, yet its return is also very low. The security represented by Y has a high return, but also has a high risk. The securities along the frontier, such as the one represented by Z,

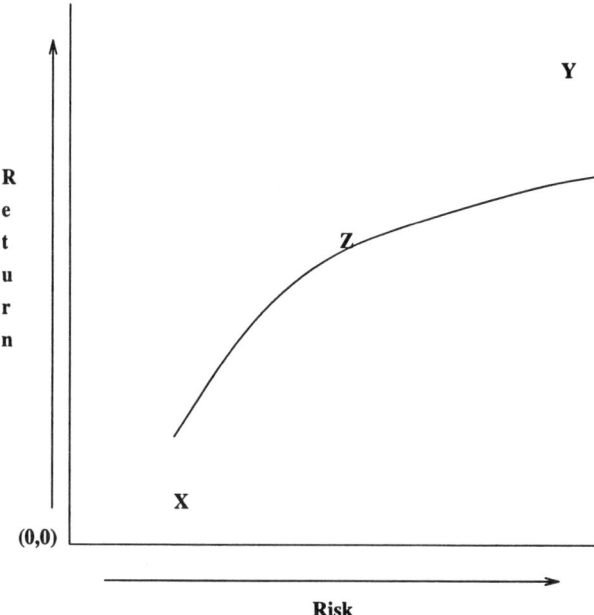

Figure 14.1: A typical risk vs. return plot.

yields the highest return for the specified level of risk. Using a risk vs. return plot, a manager can construct a portfolio geared to a specific investor's risk tolerance.

Valuation Analysis

There are three stages to the valuation of mortgage-backed securities. The first stage is the generation of a collection of interest rate scenarios. The second stage is to calculate the cash flows on each of these scenarios, and the third stage is to compute the value of the security (and the interest rate paid) based on the cash flows along the scenarios.

> A *spread* on a mortgage is an addition to an interest rate that indicates an assessment of the risk on that mortgage. An *option adjusted spread* is a spread that incorporates the value of the prepayment option on a mortgage.

14.6. Portfolio Management

1. *Generate interest rate scenarios.* There are two different methods for generating the 2^{360} interest rate scenarios. Either way, a subset of the paths, drawn from a normal distribution, is used for the valuation analysis.

    - *Monte Carlo simulation.* One method builds interest rate paths using a Monte Carlo simulation. This is similar to the stochastic path model we discussed in a previous chapter. An interest rate volatility variable is applied to a set of random numbers. The interest rate at time t is computed as a function of the volatility, the interest at time $t-1$ as well as some additional terms. These extra terms are included to make sure that the rates along the calculated interest rate path stay within historically acceptable bounds and are consistent with the interest rate structure of the underlying securities being analyzed. As was discussed earlier, path generation using this diffusion method can be trivially parallelized and is a very attractive application for parallel processing architectures.

    - *Sampling from a binomial lattice.* The other method samples paths from a *binomial lattice* (see Figure 14.2). A binomial lattice is a structure that demonstrates the possible paths through which a rate may pass. The x-axis represents time steps, and the y-axis represents different interest rate *states*. We assume that at each time step, interest rates may either move up, down, or stay the same. Interest rate movements are fitted to the binomial lattice in a way that each state represents an interest rate (which is computed as a function of the state value and a volatility associated with that state). The rates are chosen so that the model matches the present interest rate yield curve.

        Motion along points in the lattice is either "up" or "down." After a number of time periods, t, there are t possible states for the interest rate, but there are 2^t possible paths along which that rate may be reached. Interest rate scenarios may be computed by sampling paths from this binomial lattice.

2. *Generate cash flows along each interest rate scenario.* Cash flows for mortgage-backed securities are made up of three components: the interest payments on the outstanding loans, the partial payment of outstanding principal, and the projected prepayment of principal. Inter-

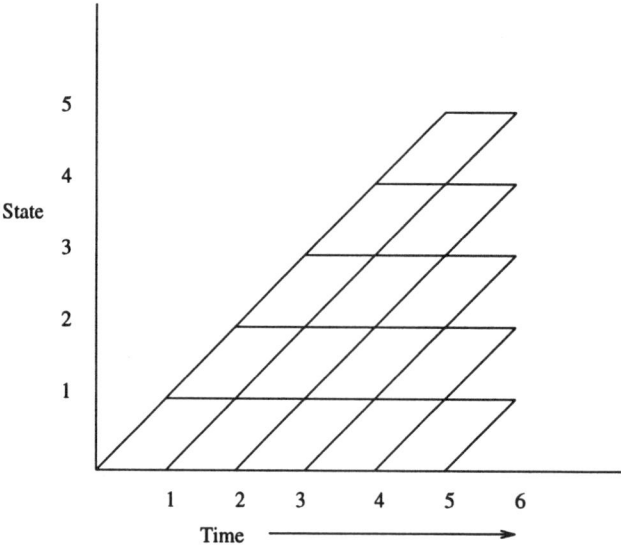

Figure 14.2: An example of a binomial lattice

est and scheduled principal payments are easily computed. The third component, prepayment of principal, is equivalent to the borrower's exercise of an option. These prepayment amounts are computed based on prediction models. If the computation of interest rate scenarios is distributed across a parallel machine, then the cash flow analysis may be distributed as well.

3. *Combine the cash flow information and the short-term interest rate information along each path.* Using the interest rate scenarios computed in the first phase and the cash flows generated in the second phase, the *option adjusted spread* is computed. The option adjusted spread incorporates the value of the prepayment option into the interest rate paid by the security.

Optimization

Now that the scenarios have been generated, the expected value of the portfolio under each scenario can be computed. The optimization problem

14.6. Portfolio Management

Portfolio Optimization

More formally, the portfolio optimization described here (which is discussed in [25], is a linear programming problem:
Maximize
$$v(\bar{x}) - \lambda\rho(\bar{x})$$
such that
$$\bar{p}^T\bar{x} \leq b,$$

$$\bar{x} \in X,$$

$$\bar{x} \geq 0$$

where $\bar{x}$ is a portfolio of asset quantities, v is the valuation, λ is the risk-aversion paramter, ρ is the risk metric function, $\bar{p}$ is the vector of asset prices, and X is a set of portfolio constraints.

then becomes one of maximizing the expected value adjusted by some risk-aversion value such that the cost of purchasing the securities falls within a given budget.

The method for performing the optimization is an iterative sequence that begins by setting the risk parameter λ to 0 (step 1) and then finding the optimal dual variables (step 2). Those variables are then checked for optimiality (step 3). If the solution is optimal, then halt; otherwise, add the solution to the linear programming system. The new system is solved (using the dual simplex method) (step 4), and the solution is then used as the starting point back at step 2.

The sequence is repeated for increasing values of the risk variable λ. Each iteration will provide portfolios with the highest return given the initial value of λ. With $\lambda = 0$, there is no risk aversion, so the resulting optimal portfolio will have high risk and high return. As λ is increased, the optimal portfolio will have lower return, but will also have lower risk. The collection of optima can be used to plot a risk-return chart similar to Figure 14.1.

14.7 Summary

Many other optimization problems map nicely to high performance and parallel computers, although the suitablity of many optimization problems to parallel procesing has not been definitely established. In the airline industry alone, airline crew pairing is just one example of the problems that may be solved using supercomputers. Many transportation related industries have similar optimization goals, such as optimal vehicle routing (similar to the traveling salesman problem), timing problems such as optimal allocation of vehicles so that certain timing constraints are met (such as railroad scheduling), and even optimal synchronization of traffic signals to provide the smoothest flow of traffic within a downtown area. The airline crew pairing problem described previously was discussed in greater detail in [4].

There is also an increase in the use of high performance systems for security pricing and portfolio analysis. The example described in this chapter was implemented on a Thinking Machines CM-2. Intel has also installed supercomputer systems with a number of Wall Street companies. Because the problem described is "embarassingly parallel," there is increasing use of networks of workstations to implement security analysis software.

Chapter 15

Graphics and Visualization

15.1 Introduction

The field of computer graphics encompasses many areas of synthetic image generation and representation. Applications of computer graphics range from modern user interface libraries (such as the Apple Macintosh interface, or X Windows), to three-dimensional modeling and rendering, as well as computer animation, interactive video editing, visualization of computed tomography scans or magnetic resonance scans, high definition television (HDTV), and virtual reality, among others.

As more computer performance is made available, the ability to make use of high performance has enhanced the techniques used and images created by computer graphics systems.

15.2 The Need for High Performance

Most graphics systems are large users of computational resources. Realistic image synthesis techniques such as *ray tracing* (described later) are computationally complex, and generating lifelike images in a reasonable time period was impossible until high performance computers were available.

Even early graphics researchers saw the need for high performance; papers published as early as 1965 describe helmets equipped with displays that presented graphical images in front of the wearer's eyes and sensors that could detect motion so as to move the display along with the user. Although the current state of the art is now moving in this direction, such as in what is now referred to as *virtual reality*, the computational needs of high speed graphics systems will devour the cycles provided by the fastest available machines.

The use of supercomputers for solving scientific problems introduces another important issue: the visualization of the physical systems being modeled. While computer graphics deals with realistic image synthesis, visualization deals with synthesis of images that are not "visible." For example, a visualization system can give a view of a DNA molecule or the way that fluids flow through porous media.

This chapter will discuss one graphics technique and then discuss the computational needs of that technique. The chapter will also include a discussion of parallelism in graphics processing, and then we will describe some advanced graphics systems that use high performance computing. Also, we will look at some issues of scientific visualization.

15.3 A Graphics Technique: Ray Tracing

Most image processing and rendering techniques are used to project three-dimensional objects onto a two-dimensional surface (see Figure 15.1). These techniques must incorporate illumination issues with visible surface information to create the two-dimensional projection.

> The *object space* consists of the abstract objects in the three-dimensional space that is being projected onto the two-dimensional place.

Illumination Models

There are basically three ways to incorporate illumination into a graphics image:

1. *The empirical model.* Empirical models try to provide an image that appears to be similar to the real image. For example, empirical models use interpolation techniques to give the appearance of smooth shading of an object.

2. *The transitional model.* Transitional models use more complex geometry to provide a more accurate appearance. For example, the true geometry of the graphical objects is taken into consideration, and greater detail is provided with respect to textures and surfaces.

15.3. A Graphics Technique: Ray Tracing

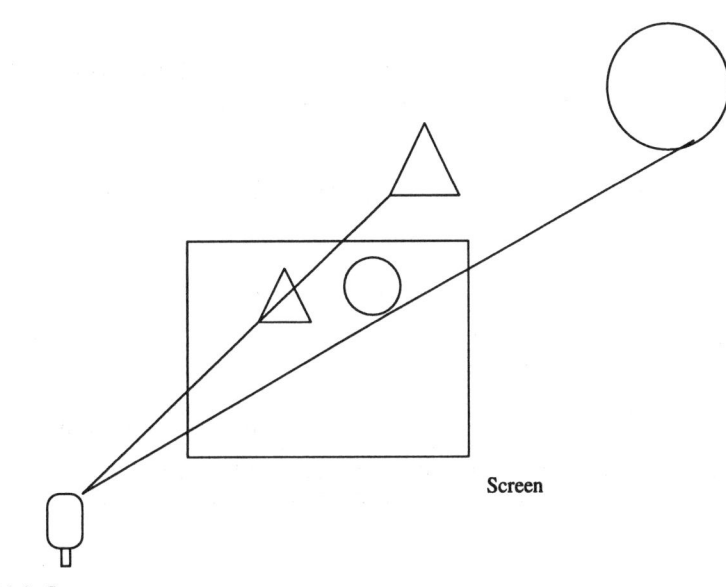

Figure 15.1: Projection onto a two-dimensional surface

3. *The analytical model.* The analytical models use the description of physical phenomena to provide an extremely realistic reproduction of the graphical image. For example, the laws of light energy and how light interacts with different types of reflective and refractive surfaces are incorporated into the analytical model.

All of the algorithms for realistic image synthesis must take into consideration that, when modeling real objects, different objects are constructed of different types of materials, which may have different degrees of opacity and reflectivity. This implies that parts of faces and edges of objects may be only partially visible in the projected image. This is called the *hidden image problem*. Because of this problem, many image synthesis algorithms compare each point in the image for its relative color and intensity by examining its illumination attributes.

All of the algorithms just mentioned will iterate over the three dimensions. For simplicity, we will examine only one algorithm, the ray tracing algorithm, in some detail to investigate its computational requirements.

A *pixel*, or picture element, is the smallest point on a display screen. A *voxel* is a volume element.

Ray Tracing

The basic idea behind the ray tracing algorithm is to consider all possible light sources and how they physically interact with each object in the object space. Rays are traced from each light source through each pixel in the two-dimensional plane and then into the object space. The object that is first hit by the ray is the one that appears in the visible surface.

When a ray projected from a light source hits a surface, a number of physical phenomena are modeled. First, any object that lies past the intersection point of the ray and the surface is in the shadow of that light source, which indicates that no light source in the shadow will contribute to the illumination of the intersection point. Second, if the material of the surface is reflective or refractive, then secondary rays are projected from the surface to model those properties. These secondary rays may then contribute to the illumination of other points in the object space. The propagation of secondary rays implies a recursive process for determining the illumination properties of each point in the object space.

15.3. A Graphics Technique: Ray Tracing

Computational Complexity of Ray Tracing

The computation of the calculations needed for ray tracing, as described in [23], are based on the intersection of rays from a particular set of light sources with objects in the object space. Any point X on a ray can be described using the equation:

$$X = P + \lambda \bar{D}, \lambda \geq 0$$

where P is the starting location of the ray, λ is the distance along the ray, and D is a direction (expressed in terms of the x, y, and z axes).

The simplest object that can be modeled, a sphere, can be described in terms of the center of the sphere and the radius to the surface. Any point X on the sphere's surface can be described by

$$|X - V| = r$$

where V is the center point, and r is the radius. By substituting the first equation into the second, and simplifying the equation, we end up with a quadratic equation:

$$\lambda^2 + (2(P - V) \times \bar{D})\lambda + (P - V)^2 - r^2 = 0$$

The solution to this equation are the points of the ray that intersect the surface of the sphere. Further manipulation of this equation will reveal that the calculation to find intersecting points involves 17 addition or subtraction operations, 17 multiplication operations, and 1 square root operation, or a total of 35 floating point operations. (For more details, see [23]).

A typical object space may contain thousands of spheres, a number of light sources, and we can assume that the surfaces of the spheres exhibit both reflective and refractive attributes (which increases the number of rays that need to be traced). Assuming a 1000 × 1000 pixel surface, 1000 spheres, and an average of 5 rays per pixel, the number of operations to determine the ray object intersections is 1000 × 1000 pixels × 5 rays per pixel × 1000 spheres per ray × 35 operations per sphere equals 175 billion floating point operations, a serious computational requirement!

The large computational requirement is not particular to ray tracing, but is inherent in any image synthesis algorithm. A way of providing the computational resources needed is to distribute the different computations to a collection of parallel processors.

15.4 Parallel Graphics Processing

The earliest use of parallelism in a graphics processing system involved pipelining the distinct phases of graphics operations. Systems developed in the 1970s by Computer Generated Imagery (CGI) broke up the computation into four pieces, and connected them together in a pipeline:

1. *The scene manager.* Object representations stored in mass storage are brought into the system by the scene manager, as well as some preliminary sorting of objects for the purpose of choosing the visible surfaces.

2. *The geometric processor.* The sorted objects are passed from the scene manager to the geometric processor. The computations for projecting the objects onto the display plane, determining which pieces of objects are actually visible in the display plane, and the color gradient are performed by the geometric processor.

3. *The video processor.* The video processor performs the hidden surface elimination and also determines the illumination and intensity values.

4. *The display.* The display is typically a high resolution graphics color monitor.

Pipelining these operations introduces a level of parallelism into graphics processing, but the performance needs of graphics systems require a higher degree of parallelism. The most extreme case would be to assign a processor to each pixel in the screen. The cost of such a system would be relatively high, and instead, systems are built where a processor is assigned to a region of the screen, representing a collection of pixels.

The 8 × 8 Display

A typical way to associate regions with a collection of processors is to build a machine with 64 processors arranged in an 8 × 8 array configuration. The screen image can then be distributed in a cyclic fashion (every eighth pixel in a row is assigned to the same processor, and every eighth pixel in a column is assigned to the same processor). This distributes the computation for each object among a collection of processors. Because some objects may be more computationally complex to render than others, this desirable cyclic allocation distributes the computational load more evenly.

15.5 Specialized Hardware: SGI's RealityEngine

The RealityEngine is a specialized graphics system designed for rendering lighted, smooth-shaded, texture-mapped objects. This system, which consists of a multiboard accelerator installed in a MIPS workstation, is a graphics pipeline machine that can treat textures as true images and not just repeating patterns.

> *Texture mapping* is the use of real-life scanned "textures" that are mapped onto surfaces in a generated image. Texture mapping is used to enhance realism. An example would be a grass texture that could be used in a flight simulator to indicate the ground. Other examples are leaves on a tree, a brick wall mapped to a virtual building, or even a label that is added to a generated package.

The RealityEngine is built as a collection of these components:

- FIFO queues.
- Command Processor.
- Geometry Engines.
- Fragment Generators.
- Image Engines.

> A *FIFO* queue, or first in, first out queue, streams in a way such that the data leaves the queue in the same order that it entered the queue.

These components are connected in a pipeline, so that input flows in through the FIFO queues into the Command Processor. The Command Processor distributes the input to any of a number of Geometry Engines. A Geometry Engine uses an Intel i860 processor to light objects, clip coordinates, project the polygons onto the window, and decompose the polygons into component triangles. The output of the Geometry Engine is streamed as input to the Fragment Generators. Data flow through the Fragment Generator in a pipeline. The Fragment Generator takes *fragments* (i.e., the triangles from the Geometry Engine) and performs rasterization, as well as performing the texture computations.

The fragments from the Fragment Generators are then distributed among the Image Engines. An Image Engine completes the image computation and maps the image into the frame buffer. The frame buffer is divided into areas, each of which is controlled by one Image Engine.

The RealityEngine can be configured with 5, 10, or 20 Fragment Generators, and 80, 160, or 320 Image Generators. This combination is a massively parallel graphics system that can render over 1 million texture mapped triangles per second, allowing for real-time image generation and interactive image processing.

15.6 Visualization

The use of graphics systems is connected very tightly to many of the high performance applications that are described in this book. The ability to model different physical systems on a computer is almost useless if the results cannot be "seen." Scientific visualization systems are incorporated into high performance applications so that the users can envision the model being simulated. The difference between graphics processing and visualization is that graphics generation is used to display accurate images, whereas visualization uses graphics techniques to display information.

> *Visualization* is the creation of visual images of things that we are unable to see or a way to display qualitative and quantitative information at a glance.

Visual images convey qualitative information with greater understanding than lists of numbers. The goal of visualization is to enable the perception of data, and the amounts of information produced by many supercomputer applications can be understood only when transformed into a visual representation.

Examples of Scientific Visualization

Some examples of the use of scientific visualization are

- Air flowing over an airplane or an automobile.

15.7. Virtual Reality

- Oil flowing through porous material.
- The atomic structure of molecules.
- The molecular structures of materials.
- Global ocean currents.
- Simulated automobile crashes.
- Climate and weather models.

Specialized Visualization Hardware: The Gigawall

A proposed visualization project at the Army High Performance Computing Research Center uses a collection of high performance computers for a large scientific visualization system called the *Gigawall*. The Gigawall is a gigapixel-per-second video wall that is 6 × 10 feet, with a screen refresh 60 times a second.

The Gigawall would allow interactive visualization by panning and zooming through a virtual reality surface. A user may is allowed to see across three dimensions (using stereo perspective glasses) from different viewpoints within those three dimensions, including from within the volume!

The Gigawall would use multiple RealityEngines, MasPar MP-2s, TMC's Connection Machines, or Ncube-2s hooked together through a HiPPI or ATM network to a high speed collection of disk arrays for I/O. For greater details about the Gigawall, see [59].

15.7 Virtual Reality

Virtual reality is a technology designed to allow a person to be surrounded by a three-dimensional computer generated environment in which that person may experience a "virtual world." This virtual world may be enhanced by interactive devices that provide a combination of visual, tactile, and aural stimuli.

Virtual reality (VR) technology is useful in a number of applications:

- *Scientific visualization.* Virtual reality assists scientists in the qualitative analysis and interpretation of large amounts of data.

- *Education.* A well known educational use of a virtual reality system is the training of pilots using flight simulators.

- *Operation in hazardous environments.* Connecting a virtual reality system to remote robotic devices allows operation in environments that are dangerous to human exposure, such as a nuclear waste spill that needs to be cleaned.

- *Virtual surgery.* A virtual reality system connected to robot mechanisms may enable surgeons to perform operations from remote locations.

- *Games.* An entertainment experience may be enhanced when the player takes a more interactive role. Virtual reality allows the player to exist within the game world.

Parallelism in Virtual Reality

There are different levels of opportunities for parallelism in virtual reality systems:

- *Environments.* Different environments may be simulated in parallel.

- *Objects.* Different objects within an environment may be rendered in parallel.

- *Attributes.* Each object may consist of smaller pieces combined. There is an opportunity to parallelize the computations for the different attributes of an object.

The CAVE

The **CAVE** is a virtual reality project that is under investigation at the National Center for Supercomputer Applications (NCSA). CAVE is an acronym for "CAVE Automatic Virtual Environment." The CAVE is a three-dimensional virtual reality theater that was originally designed for scientific visualization. It was planned to be a $10 \times 10 \times 10$ theater, with three

15.7. Virtual Reality

rear projection walls and a down projection floor. The walls and floor consist of high resolution (1280 × 1024 24-bit image pixels) color images created by high performance workstations built by Silicon Graphics. The CAVE developed out of the desire to break away from the monitor-based graphics and visualization systems into a more interactive, inclusive (or "inside-out") medium for visualization.

The CAVE is designed so that a user may interact directly inside a three-dimensional environment. The CAVE uses a cube to simulate the "feel" of being encompassed by a sphere (which is similar to the better known Omnimax theaters). The designers of the CAVE leveraged the technology of projected three-dimensional objects onto a two-dimensional surface to "merge" the edges along the wall seams to give the feel of the sphere. Special glasses are worn, which in tandem with the projected stereo images, allows the user to see three-dimensional objects. Synchronized screen updates attempt to reduce the amount of flicker. Because the three image walls are rear-projected, they cast no shadows, but shadows are produced across the down projected floor. There CAVE has electromagnetic trackers to track the motion of the users inside

The CAVE is a true marriage of graphics applications, high speed networks, and high performance computing. According to [14], the amount of computing power needed to perform real time continuous update for complex models exceeds by far the computing power available today. To provide a flicker-free scene, the image must be updated 60 times a second. To transmit one wall image of the CAVE 60 times a second requires almost 2 gigabits of network throughput. This must be done for four wall surfaces!

The CAVE is an ongoing research project; some of the issues currently being investigated include projection on all six sides of the cube, lowering the cost of construction, and increased robustness to allow models to be built for less controlled environments (such as museums or schools). The CAVE was debuted at the SIGGRAPH 1992 conference and was also set up at the Supercomputing 1992 conference.

Part VI

Availability

Chapter 16

Conclusion

16.1 Timely, Timeless, or What?

Computer technology advances at a very fast pace. Every two years the speed of the fastest computers doubles. Because of this fast pace of development, no book can capture the world of high performance computing without the risk of becoming obsolete.

On the other hand, we have attempted to give an idea about the world of high performance computing, and the nature by which state-of-the-art supercomputer applications migrate into the mainstream.

Today's workstations are as powerful as the fastest supercomputers of twenty years ago. Currently, the promise of parallel processing is brought to the desktop as reasonably priced superpipelined microprocessors and symmetric multiprocessor accelerator boards are introduced for personal computers. As these machine architectures move from the cutting edge to the office desktop, they lose their status as "supercomputers."

Because of the rapidly evolving nature of the industry, it is impossible to cover all high performance applications or to discuss all high perfromance architectures. To help the reader keep track of future developments in the world of high performance computing, a list of sources of information is provided.

16.2 National Laboratories

The following is a list of national laboratories that have supercomputer facilities. Many of these laboratories allocate supercomputer time to non-

> **NCSA Mosaic**
>
> NCSA Mosaic is an information retrieval and display tool that supports the World Wide Web. NCSA Mosaic, which was authored at the National Center for Supercomputer Applications at the University of Illinois, is a hypertext information browser that can be used to "travel along the information highway." Information is retrieved via URL requests for data transfer from remote sites located on the World Wide Web, an international network of accessible information.
>
> NCSA Mosaic is available in versions for X Windows, Microsoft Windows, and the Apple Macintosh. The NCSA Mosaic software can be obtained via anonymous FTP from `ftp.ncsa.uiuc.edu`, in the directory /Web.
>
> Information about high performance computing centers and vendors can be accessed using NCSA Mosaic. When available, the NCSA Mosaic home pages for references in this chapter will be noted.

employee researchers. Contact the specific laboratory for information regarding applications for computer time.

- *Argonne National Laboratory, High-Performance Computing Research Facility.* The Argonne National Laboratory is run by the Department of Energy, and is operated by University of Chicago. Argonne's High-Performance Computing Research Facility (HPCRF) includes a number of multiprocessor machines, including an IBM SP-1, BBN TC2000, and Intel iPSC/860. Access is provided to an Intel Paragon machine at Caltech through the Concurrent Supercomputing Consortium.

    Argonne National Laboratory
    9700 S. Cass Ave.
    Argonne, IL 60439

- *Lawrence Livermore National Laboratory.* The Lawrence Livermore National Laboratory's high performance computing facility includes a Meiko CS-2. It is being used in the definition of the Livermore model, a massively parallel environment used for capability and capacity computing on a machine that can be run using multiple parallel

16.2. National Laboratories

programming styles. Also, researchers at Livermore's National Storage Laboratory explore issues in high performance storage environments and scalable I/O.

Lawrence Livermore National Laboratory
University of California
Livermore, CA 94550

- *Los Alamos National Laboratory.* The Department of Energy's Los Alamos National Laboratory is the home of the High Performance Computing Research Center and the Advanced Computing Laboratory.

Los Alamos National Laboratory
Department of Energy
Los Alamos, New Mexico 87545

- *Oak Ridge National Laboratory.* Managed by Martin Marietta Energy Systems, Inc., the Oak Ridge National Laboratory's ORNAL Center for Computational Sciences has a KSR1, Intel Paragon, among others. ORNAL provides resources for Grand Challenge computing. An ongoing project at Oak Ridge is CHAMMP: Computer Hardware, Advanced Mathematics and Model Physics, where researchers investigate advanced models for climate research.

Oak Ridge National Laboratory
Oak Ridge, TN 37831-6367

- *NERSC - National Energy Research Supercomputer Center.* Located at Livermore, NERSC has access to resources at Oak Ridge and Los Alamos.

National Energy Research Supercomputer Center
Lawrence Livermore National Laboratory
University of California
Livermore, CA 94550

- *Sandia National Laboratory.* Sandia is the home of the Massively Parallel Computing Research Lab, where work is done on mesh generation, molecular dynamics, and quantum electronics. Sandia has a 1840 node Intel Paragon.

- *Army HPC Research Center, Minnesota Supercomputer Center, Inc.* The objective of research at AHPCRC (run by the Department of Defense) is the integration of heterogeneous supercomputer resources into one environment, such as connecting a Cray-2, a CM-5, a CM-200, and SGI mchines via HIPPI to support three-dimensional dataset visualization.

  http://www.arc.umn.edu/html/ahpcrc.html

  Army High Performance Computing Research Center
  Institute of Technology
  Suite 101
  1100 Washington Avenue South
  Minneapolis, MN 55415

- *NASA Langley.* The focal point for activities at NASA's Langley Research Center is in mathematical and numerical analysis, and scientific and engineering applications.

  Institute for Computer Applications in Science and Engineering (ICASE)
  NASA Langley Research Center
  Hampton, VA 23665-5225

  http://www.icase.edu/docs/home.html

- *NASA Ames Research.* The Numerical Aerodynamic Simulation Division is situated at NASA's Ames Research Center. The focus of research is computational fluid dynamics and computational aerospace applications using a Cray-90, a CM-5, a Paragon, two Convex 3820s, and assorted SGI machines.

  Numerical Aerodynamic Simulation Division
  NASA Ames Research Center
  Moffett Field, CA 94035-1000

  http:/www.nas.nasa.gov/home.html

The following lists the National Science Foundation (NSF) supercomputer centers.

16.2. National Laboratories

- *Cornell Theory Center.* One of the NSF centers, the Theory Center makes use of an IBM ES/9000, an SP1, a RS/6000 Parallel Cluster, and a KSR1 from Kendall Square Research. The Theory Center is a beta site for IBM's POWER Visualization System (PVS, DataExplorer (DX)) software. Also, research at the Theory Center focuses on issues of parallel programming tools.

    Cornell Theory Center
    514 Engineering and Theory Center Building
    Hoy Road
    Ithaca, NY 14853-3801
    consult@tc.cornell.edu

    http://www.tc.cornell.edu/ctc.html

- *NCAR - National Center for Atmospheric Research.* Part of the National Consortium for High Performance Computing and funded by ARPA, NCAR's Scientific Computing Division provides supercomputing resources for research in atmospheric, oceanic, and related sciences.

    National Center for Atmospheric Research
    Scientific Computing Division
    P.O. Box 3000
    Boulder, Colorado 80307-3000

    http://http.ucar.edu/metapage.html

- *NCSA: National Center for Supercomputing Applications.* Research at NCSA focuses on building applications that make use of high performance computers. The resources available at NCSA include a CM-5, a CM-2, a Convex C-3, a Cray-2, and a Cray Y-MP.

    National Center for Supercomputing Applications (NCSA)
    152 Computing Applications Building
    605 East Springfield Avenue
    Champaign, IL 61820-5518
    consult@ncsa.uiuc.edu

    http://www.ncsa.uiuc.edu/General/NCSAIntro.html

- *Pittsburgh Supercomputing Center.* Among the machines at PSC are a Cray C-90, CM-2, CM-5, and a DEC RISC cluster. Application-based research and development at PSC covers computational chemistry and molecular structure determination, as well as neural sciences.

    Pittsburgh Supercomputing Center
    Mellon Institute Building 4400 Fifth Avenue
    Pittsburgh, PA 15213-2683
    remarks@psc.edu

    http://pscinfo.psc.edu/

- *San Diego Supercomputer Center.* Resources at SDSC include machines from nCUBE, Intel, Alliant, and Cray. Research at SDSC includes fusion energy and biomedical applications.

    San Diego Supercomputer Center (SDSC)
    10100 John J. Hopkins Drive
    San Diego, CA 92037
    consult@y1.sdsc.edu

    http://gopher.sdsc.edu/Home.html

More information can be found at the URL
http://www.nersc.gov/doc/Parallel_Processing/Brent/brentpp.html or http://pscinfo.psc.edu/MetaCenter/MetaInfo.html.

16.3 Hard Copy Publications

Here is a list of publications that provide information about high performance computers, applications, and the industry in general:

- Communications of the ACM
  P.O. Box 12114
  Church Street Station
  New York, NY 10257

16.3. Hard Copy Publications

- High Performance Computing and Communications Week
  King Communications Corp.
  627 National Press Building
  Washington, DC 20045

- High Performance Computing Review
  12416 Hymeadow Drive
  Austin, TX 78750-1986

- IEEE Computer
  10662 Los Vaqueros Circle
  P.O. Box 3014
  Los Alamitos, CA 90720-1264

- IEEE Parallel and Distributed Computing
  10662 Los Vaqueros Circle
  P.O. Box 3014
  Los Alamitos, CA 90720-1264

- IEEE Parallel and Distributed Technology
  10662 Los Vaqueros Circle
  P.O. Box 3014
  Los Alamitos, CA 90720-1264

- International Journal of Supercomputing Applications
  MIT Press Journals
  55 Hayward St.
  Cambridge, MA 02142

- Journal of Parallel and Distributed Computing
  Academic Press, Inc.
  6277 Sea Harbor Drive
  Orlando, FL 32887-4900

- Microprocessor Report
  874 Gravenstein Hwy. So.
  Suite 14
  Sebastopol, CA 95472

- Parallelogram
  16 Langley Road
  Durham, NH 03824-3424

- Spang Robinson Report on High Performance Computing
  Customer Service
  John Wiley & Sons, Inc.
  Subscription Department
  605 Third Avenue
  New York, NY 10158-0012

16.4 Online Information

An online publication entitled *HPCwire* is sent to subscribers weekly via email. Subscription information may be obtained by sending email to
    sub@hpcwire.ans.net.
The following lists some Internet newsgroups dedicated to high performance computing mentioned in this book:

- comp.compilers

- comp.parallel

- comp.parallel.mpi

- comp.parallel.pvm

- somp.sys.isis

- comp.sys.super

Information on PVM can be obtained via anonymous FTP from netlib2.cs.utk.edu.

16.5 Manufacturers

A number of different high performance computer and software providers have been mentioned in this book. To learn more about their products, you can write to them at the addresses listed below.

- Convex Computer Corp.
  3000 Waterview Pkwy.
  Richardson, TX 75080

- Cray Research, Inc.
  655A Lone Oak Dr.
  Eagan, MN 55121

- Digital Equipment Corporation
  High Performance Computing Group
  129 Parker Street
  Maynard, MA 01754

- Hewlett-Packard Co.
  3000 Hanover St.
  Palo Alto, CA 94303

  or

  Hewlett-Packard Workstation Systems Division
  300 Apollo Dr.
  Chelmsford, MA 01824

- Informix Corp.
  4100 Bohannon Dr.
  Menlo Park, CA 94025

- International Business Machines Corporation
  1133 Westchester Avenue
  White Plains, NY 10604

- Intel Supercomputer Systems Division
  15201 N.W. Greenbrier Parkway
  Beaverton, OR 97006

- Kendall Square Research
  170 Tracer Ln.
  Waltham, MA 02154

- MasPar Computer Corp.
  749 North Mary Ave.
  Sunnyvale, CA 94086

- Meiko Scientific Corp.
  Waltham, MA 02154

- NCR
  1700 South Patterson Blvd.
  Dayton, OH 45479

- nCUBE, Inc.
  919 East Hillsdale Blvd.
  Foster City, CA 94404

- Oracle Systems Corporation
  500 Oracle Parkway
  Redwood City, CA 94065

- Sequent Computer Systems, Inc.
  15450 Southwest Koll Pkwy.
  Beaverton, OR 97006

- Silicon Graphics, Inc.
  2011 Northshore Blvd.
  Mountain View, CA 94039

16.5. Manufacturers

- Stratus Computer Inc.
  55 Fairbanks Blvd.
  Marlborough, MA 01752

- Sybase, Inc.
  6475 Christie Ave.
  Emeryville, CA 94608

- Tandem Computers, Inc.
  19333 Vallco Parkway
  Cupertino, CA 95014

- Thinking Machines Corporation
  245 First St.
  Cambridge, MA 02142

Glossary

This is a collection of commonly used terms in the high performance world. Many of these terms were used in the preceding chapters.

- **Achievable performance.** This is the expected maximum speed that a computer may attain. This number is derived based on the peak performance of the machine and the features that prevent the peak from being reached.

- **Array processor.** An array of specialized processing elements that are networked together and operate under the control of a single control processor.

- **ATM.** An acronym for asynchronous transfer mode, a message passing mechanism. A network that uses ATM is meant to provide higher bandwidth than networks that use a synchronous transfer mode.

- **Bandwidth.** The capacity of a network measured in units per time period.

- **C*.** A data parallel programming language originally designed for programming the Connection Machine.

- **Cache.** A fast hardware memory module that is used to automatically keep frequently used data "close" to the processor, to minimize the cost of bring the data into CPU registers.

- **Cache coherence.** Maintenance of consistent copies of data items in caches in a shared memory multiprocessor system.

- **Client-server model.** A server is a group of (one or more) cooperating processes that provide a service to a group of users, called *clients*.

- **Communications library.** In a multiprocessor system programmed using a message passing model, data is transferred by calling functions from a communications library.

- **Compiler.** A program that transforms a program written in a high level language into another form. Compilers most often transform programs into the machine code for the machine targeted for execution. See Chapter 8.

- **CPU.** An acronym for central processing unit, the "brains" of a computer.

- **Daemon.** A special operating system process that stays resident and performs system level operations for a user when requested or carries out unnoticed system tasks.

- **Distributed memory.** A multiple processor system has a distributed memory system if every processor may only access data from an assigned pool of addresses. In a distributed memory system, data are shared through messages. Compare to shared memory.

- **Discretization.** The replacement of a set of equations that hold over a continuous set of points in a coordinate system into a collection of equations related to the original set, but defined over selected i.e., discrete, points in the coordinate system.

- **Floating point.** Floating point arithmetic is how a machine computes operations over a representation of real numbers (as opposed to integer numbers).

- **Fault tolerance.** The ability of a system to continue its operation in the presence of a failure of one or more components. For example, a distributed system consisting of a network of workstations that can continue operation when up to three of the workstations fail is said to be tolerant of three faults.

- **Finite difference method.** A method for solving partial differential equations.

- **Finite element method.** A method for solving partial differential equations.

Glossary

- **FLOPS.** An acronym that stands for floating point operations per second, used as a measurement of speed of floating point processing.

- **Fortran.** A high level programming language often used for scientific applications, among others. Derivations of Fortran are used as the language of choice for programming many high performance machines.

- **GigaFLOPS.** *Giga* is a prefix meaning 1 billion, or 10^9; GFLOPS or GigaFLOPS means billion floating point operations per second. See FLOPS.

- **HiPPI.** An acronym for high performance parallel interface. A HiPPI interface is a high speed network interconnection interface.

- **LRU.** An acronym for least recently used, a resource replacement strategy that is used to choose one resource from a pool of resources as a victim to be replaced. LRU is used for memory page replacement, as well as for cache line replacement.

- **Matrix.** A multidimensional array.

- **Message passing.** In a multiple process application, information may be relayed from one process to another process through the use of message passing. If each process has been allocated to a specific processor in a multiprocessor system, the message passing system must use a network to send and receive messages.

- **MFLOPS or MegaFLOPS.** The *mega* prefix denotes 1 million, or 10^6; MFLOPS stands for million floating point operations per second.

- **MPP.** An acronym for massively parallel processing. An MPP machine incorporates a "large" number of processors in a network. *Large number* is a term that is contested; some industry people claim 32 processors can make up an MPP system, while others would argue that a much larger number of processors is required.

- **Microcode.** The hardware-encoded low level instructions that indicate how specific machine instructions are to be computed.

- **MIMD.** An acronym for multiple instruction multiple data. A MIMD computer is a machine with multiple processors in which the flow of control at one processor is different from the control flow at another processor, and different computations may be done on different data in parallel. Compare to SIMD.

- **MIPS.** An acronym for millions of instructions per second. This is a quantification of speed of a processor; e.g., the i860-XR processor operates at 100 MIPS.

- **MISD.** An acronym for multiple instruction stream, single data stream. This is the category of machines with a collection of processors that execute different instruction streams on one data stream.

- **Multicomputer.** A computer composed of multiple processors; the processors share data through shared memory.

- **Multiple instruction issue.** A microprocessor than has the capacity for initiating more than one intruction on each clock cycle is called a multiple instruction issue machine.

- **Multiprocessor.** A computer composed of multiple processors; the processors share data through message-passing.

- **Mutual exclusion.** The act of locking out all other accesses to an object when it is being updated by a particular writer is referred to as mutual exclusion.

- **Network.** A communications pathway through which attached processing nodes can send messages.

- **OLTP.** An acronym for on line transaction processing.

- **Optimization.** A mechanism for achieving better performance while retaining correctness of a process.

- **Parallelism.** The state of more than one simultaneous events occurring, most often used to describe concurrent computation.

- **Parallelization.** A mechanism implemented in compilers to recognize a collection of operations that may be executed in parallel.

- **PC, or program counter.** A register that holds the memory address of the next instruction to be executed in a program.

Glossary

- **Peak performance.** The absolute maximum speed that the machine can run. This maximum is dictated by physical bounds, such as the speed of the processor and the number of operations that may be performed at any time.

- **Pipeline.** A multiple step process in which partial results are made available at specific time steps and then passed along to the next step in the process.

- **Prefetch.** A request to the memory system to read data into a cache before it is actually needed. The prefetch, when used in a consistent manner, will provide greater memory to processor bandwidth.

- **Programming model.** The model of a paradigm of computation that may occur on a machine. For example, programming an application to execute on a multiple processor system with independent processes running on different processors that interact by sending and receiving messages is an example of a message-passing programming model.

- **PVM.** An acronym for Parallel Virtual Machine, a message-passing library and programming environment that allows users to build cooperative applications across multiple hardware platforms.

- **RISC.** An acronym for reduced instruction set computer, a class of processors whose instruction sets are limited to a small collection of fast and necessary instructions.

- **Scalability.** A term used to infer assertions about a system through the addition of similar resources.

- **Scoreboard.** A hardware embellishment added to fast processors to keep track of the definition and use of different CPU resources (such as register values). A scoreboard is used to indicate to the CPU that a certain register result from a previous instruction may not yet be available and the CPU must stall the beginning of execution of an instruction that uses this register result.

- **Shared memory.** A multiple processor system has a shared memory system if every processor has the ability to access any memory address in the system. Compare to distributed memory.

- **SIMD.** An acronym for single instruction multiple data. A SIMD machine is a multiple processor machine in which the computation performed is identical at each processor, although the computation is performed on different data. Compare to MIMD.

- **SISD.** An acronym for single instruction stream, single data stream. Conventional sequential computers fall into this category, where a single processing unit executes a sequential stream of operations on a single stream of data.

- **SMP.** An acronym for shared memory processor. This is a computer with multiple processors that are loosely coupled with ports to a multi-ported shared memory.

- **Speedup.** The ratio of increase in performance to increase in number of processors.

- **SPMD.** An acronym for single program, multiple data. The SPMD programming model assumes that a single program is instantiated at all processors in a multiple processor system, but each the execution of that program (potentially) proceeds independently on different processors.

- **Superscalar.** A processor that can execute more than one instruction per clock cycle.

- **Software pipelining.** A technique for reordering the operations within a loop such that each operation within the software pipelined loop is chosen from a different iteration of the originally specified loop.

- **Switch.** A hardware device used to reroute data along a communication line.

- **TeraFLOPS.** *Tera* is a prefix meaning 1 trillion, or 10^{12}; TFLOPS or TeraFLOPS means trillion floating point operations per second.

- **Vector.** A representation of a set of data, usually as a multidimensional array. Often vectors are assumed to be one dimensional.

- **Vectorization.** A mechanism implemented in compilers to recognize operations performed on vectors, and representing the vector operation in an equivalent representation.

Glossary

- **Vector processing.** A term that describes the logical operations performed on a set of vector operands. Vector processing is often described in the context of vector processing machines. These machines have the capacity to efficiently compute vector operations through special hardware enhancements. For more details, see Chapter 5.

- **VLIW.** An acronym for very long instruction word. A VLIW processor has wide instruction word size that allows for multiple operations to be requested at one time.

Bibliography

[1] Hojjat Adeli, editor *'Supercomputing in Engineering Analysis,'* Marcel Dekker Inc., New York, NY.

[2] Kurt Akeley, 'RealityEngine Graphics,' *SIGGRAPH 93 Conference Proceedings*, ACM Press, New York, NY, 1993.

[3] George S. Almasi, Allan J Gottlieb, *'Highly Parallel Computing,'* Benjamin/Cummings Publishing Company, Inc., Redwood City, CA, 1989.

[4] R. Anbil, R. Tangua, E. L. Johnson, 'A Global Approach to Crew Pairing Optimization,' *IBM Systems Journal*, Vol. 31, No. 1, 1992.

[5] M. A. Arbib and J. A. Robinson, *'Natural and Artificial Parallel Computation,'* MIT Press, Cambridge, MA, 1990.

[6] Richard S. Barr and Betty L. Hickman, 'Parallel Simplex for Large Pure Network Problems: Computational Testing and Sources of Speedup,' Operations Research, 1993.

[7] Dimitri P. Bertsekas, *'Linear Network Optimization Algorithms and Codes,'* MIT Press, Cambridge, Massachusetts, 1991.

[8] Bruce M. Boghosian, 'Lattice Gas Hydrodynamics,' *Nuclear Physics B*, Vol. 30, 1993.

[9] C. Brandon and J. Toole, *'Introduction to Protein Structure,'* Garland Publishing, Inc, 1991.

[10] C. A. Brebbia, A. Peters, editors, *'Applications of Supercomputers in Engineering: Fluid Flow and Stress Analysis Applications,'* Computational Mechanics Publications, Southampton, UK, 1989.

[11] Leigh D. Cagan, 'How to Make the Most of Financial Codes,' *High Performance Computing Review*, May/June 1993.

[12] Maureen Caudill, *'Neural Networks Primer,'* AI Expert, Boulder CO, third edition 1993.

[13] J.J. Connor and C.A. Brebbia, *'Finite Element Techniques for Fluid Flow,'* Newnes-Butterworths, 1976.

[14] Carolina Cruz-Neira, Daniel J. Sandin, Thomas A. DeFanti, 'Surround-Screen Projection-Based Virtual Reality: The Design and Implementation of the CAVE,' *SIGGRAPH 93 Conference Proceedings*, ACM Press, New York, NY, 1993.

[15] Martin de Prycker, *'Asynchronous Transfer Mode Solution for Broadband ISDN,'* Ellis Norwood Limited, Chichester, West Sussex, England, 1991.

[16] Mark Hull Dobson, personal communication.

[17] R. A. Earnshaw, M. A. Gigante, H. Jones, editors, *'Virtual Reality Systems,'* Academic Press, San Diego, CA, 1993.

[18] Dror G. Feitelson, Peter F. Corbett, Sandra Johnson Baylor, Yarsun Hsu, 'Satisfying the Secondary Storage Requirements of Massively Parallel Supercomputers,' 1993.

[19] Geoffrey C. Fox, 'Domain Decomposition in Distributed and Shared Memory Environments,' Invited Paper at International Conference on Supercomputing 87, 1987.

[20] Al Geist, Adam Beguelin, Jack Dongarra, Weicheng Jiang, Robert Manchek, Vaidy Sunderam, *'PVM 3 User's Guide and Reference Manual,'* ORNL/TM-12187, Oak Ridge National Laboratory, Oak Ridge, TN, 1993.

[21] Maria V. Georgianis, 'Locking In The Transaction,' *Computer Reseller News*, February 1, 1993.

[22] David E. Goldberg, *'Genetic Algorithms in Search, Optimization, and Machine Learning,'* Addison-Wesley, Reading, MA, 1989.

[23] Stuart Green, *'Parallel Processing for Computer Graphics,'* MIT Press, Cambridge, MA, 1991.

Bibliography

[24] John L. Hennessy and David A. Patterson, *'Computer Architecture–A Quantitative Approach,'* Morgan Kaufman Publishers, Inc., San Mateo, CA, 1990.

[25] Randall S. Hiller, Jonathan Eckstein, 'Stochastic Dedication: Designing Fixed Income Portfolios Using Massively Parallel Benders Decomposition,' *Management Science*, Vol. 39, No. 11, November 1993.

[26] R. W. Hockney and C. R. Jesshope, *'Parallel Computers 2,'* Adam Hilger, Bristol and Philadelphia, IOP Publishing, Bristol, UK, 1988.

[27] HPC Select News (*for information, send electronic mail to sub@hpcwire.ans.net.*

[28] James M. Hutchinson, Stavros A. Zenios, 'Financial Simulations on a Massively Parallel Connection Machine,' Technical Report FA90-1, Thinking Machines Corporation, Cambridge, MA, 1990.

[29] Kai Hwang, *'Supercomputers: Design and Applications,'* IEEE Computer Society Press, Silver Spring, MD, 1984.

[30] Kai Hwang and Faye A. Briggs, *'Computer Architecture and Parallel Processing,'* McGraw-Hill, New York, NY, 1984.

[31] Josh Hyatt, 'SuperMarketing,' *Boston Globe*, Boston, MA, February 28, 1993.

[32] Robert Jones, 'Protein Sequence and Structure Comparison on Massively Parallel Computers,' *The International Journal of Supercomputer Applications*, Vol. 6, No. 2, Summer 1992.

[33] Robert Jones, 'Sequence Pattern Matching on a Massively Parallel Computer,' *Cabios*, Vol. 8. No. 4, Oxford University Press, 1992.

[34] William J. Kaufmann III, Larray L. Smarr, *'Supercomputing and the Transformation of Science,'* Scientific American Library, W. H. Freeman and Company, New York, NY, 1993.

[35] J.R. Kirkland, J.H. Poore, editors, *'Supercomputers–A Key to U.S. Scientific, Technological, and Industrial Preeminence,'* Praeger Publishers, New York, NY, 1987.

[36] Charles H. Koelbel, David B. Loveman, Robert S. Schreiber, Guy L. Steele, Jr., Mary E. Zosel, *'The High Performance Fortran Handbook,'* MIT Press, Cambridge, MA, 1994.

[37] Charles E. Leiserson, Zahi S. Abuhamdeh, David C. Douglas, Carl R. Feynman, Mahesh N. Ganmukhi, Jeffrey V. Hill, W. Daniel Hillis, Bradley C. Kuszmaul, Margaret A. St. Pierre, David S. Wells, Monica C. Wong, Shaw-Wen Yang, and Robert Zak, 'The Network Architecture of the Connection Machine CM-5,' *4th Symposium on Parallel Algorithms and Architecture*, 1992.

[38] Wm Leler, 'Linda Meets Unix,' IEEE Computer, February, 1990.

[39] Danial Lenoski, James Laudon, Kourosh Gharachorloo, Wolf-Dietrich Weber, Anoop Gupta, John Hennessy, Mark Horowitz, and Monica S. Lam, 'The Stanford Dash Multiprocesor,' *IEEE Computer*, March, 1992.

[40] Garth P. McCormick, *'Nonlinear Programming, Theory Algorithms and Applications,'* Wiley-Interscience, John Wiley and Sons, 1983.

[41] James L. McClelland, David E. Rumelhart, and the PDP Research Group, 'Parallel Distributed Processing,' Vol. 1 and Vol. 2, MIT Press, 1988.

[42] Raul H. Mendez, editor, *'Visualization in Supercomputing,'* Springer-Verlag, New Yowk, NY, 1990.

[43] Jill Mesirov, editor, *'WLSC 21 Very Large Scale Computation in the 21st Century,'* Society for Industrial and Applied Mathematics, Philadelphia, PA, 1991.

[44] Lynn Nadel, Daniel L. Stein, editors, *'1990 Lectures in Complex Systems,'* Addison-Wesley, Redwood City, CA, 1990.

[45] T. A. J. Nicholson, *'Optimization in Industry, Volume II Industrial Applications,'* T. and A. Constable Ltd., Edinburgh, 1971.

[46] Troy Nolan, 'A Personal Approach to Parallel Processing,' *High Performance Computing Review*, March, 1993.

[47] D. A. Patterson, Garth Gibson, Randy Katz, 'A Case for Redundant Arrays of Inexpensive Disks,' Proceedings of SIGMOD 1988, ACM Press, New York, NY, 1988.

Bibliography

[48] G. Robertson, 'Parallel Implementation of Genetic Algorithms in a Classifier System,' Thinking Machines Corporation Technical Report RL87-5.

[49] Rogers and Kabrisky, *'An Introduction to Biologial and Artificial Neural Networks for Pattern Recognition,'* SPIE Optical Engineering Press, Bellingham, Washington.

[50] Rolf Sabersky and Allen Acosta, *'Fluid Flow A First Course in Fluid Mechanics,'* Collier MacMillan Limited, New York, NY.

[51] R. E. Sheriff and L. P. Geldart, *'Exploration Seismology Volume 2, Data-processing and Interpretation,'* Cambridge University Press, Cambridge, UK, 1983.

[52] Karl Sims, 'Artificial Evolution for Computer Graphics,' *Computer Graphics,* Volume 25, Number 4, 1991.

[53] Karl Sims, 'Interactive Evolution of Equations for Procedural Models,' 1992.

[54] C. Stanfil, 'Memory-Based Reasoning Applied to English Pronunciation,' Thinking Machines Corporation Technical Report RL87-4.

[55] Andrew S. Tanenbaum, *'Modern Operating Systems,'* Prentice Hall, Englewood Cliffs, NJ, 1992.

[56] Alan Wexelblat, editor, *'Virtual Reality Applications and Explorations,'* Academic Press Professional, Boston, MA, 1993.

[57] Michael Witbrock and Marco Zagha, 'An Implementation of Back Propagation Learning on GF11, a Large SIMD Parallel Computer,' *Parallel Computing,* 14, 1990.

[58] Michael Wolfe, *'Optimizing Supercompilers for Supercomputers,'* MIT Press, Cambridge, MA, 1989.

[59] Paul R. Woodward, 'Interactive Scientific Visualization of Fluid Flow,' *IEEE Computer,* October, 1993.

[60] Ozdogan Yilmaz, *'Seismic Data Processing,'* Society of Exploration Geophysicists, Tulsa, OK, 1987.

Index

8 × 8 display 218

α-helix 170

β-strand 170

Active Messages 134
Advanced Regional Prediction System 156
Advanced Scientific Computer (TI) 64
AI 10, 169, 174, 177, 181
airplane 143, 153–154
ALL 111
allocatable arrays 109
ALLOCATE (Fortran 90 statement) 109
ALLOCATED 111
Alpha 20, 37, 92, 94
American Express 184
amino acids 170–171
Amoco 167
Amoeba 133
analysis metrics 7, 239
animation 5, 181
anitdependence 129
ANY 111
Apple Computers 41
Arco 167
Argonne National Laboratory 228
Army HPC Research Center 230
ARPS 156

array construction intrinsics 111
array inquiry intrinsics 111
array location intrinsics 111
array manipulation intrinsics 111
array processor 61, 66, 68, 70, 239
array sections 109–110
artificial intelligence 10, 169, 174, 177, 181
artificial life 10, 179–181
asynchronous transfer mode 57, 93, 239
ASC 64
ATM 57, 93, 239
attached array processor 61, 66, 68, 70
automatic parallelization 123, 126–127, 191, 242
automatic vectorization 123–124, 244
automobile 6, 143, 144, 154, 155
axon 174

bandwidth 45, 53, 56, 57, 93, 94, 239
Barclays Bank 190
basis 203
Benes network
binomial lattice 209
biochemistry 169
biology 169
Birman, Ken 139
Black, Fisher 189

Black–Scholes model 189
block distribution 114, 193
block-cyclic distribution 114
BSP 17, 70
Burroughs Scientific 68, 70
Burroughs Scientific Processor 17, 70

C 124
C* 115, 239
    context 115
    get 116–117
    parallel variable 115
    pccord 116
    send 116–117
    shape 115, 116
cache 13, 30, 33–38, 239
cache coherence 76–81, 239
    directory-based 79
    snoopy-based 79
California Institute of Technology 20
CAPS 156
CART 187
CAVE 222
cash flow 207, 209
CDC 16, 65–66
CDP 161, 165
cellular automata 179–180
Center for Analysis and Prediction of Storms 156
CGI 218
chromosomes 169
CISC 26, 27, 29, 37
Classification and Regression Trees 187
client-server 132–133, 138, 184, 185, 240
clock 26, 28

cluster of workstations 91
coherence 164
collection of workstations 91
Coloumb's law 173
combining functions 46, 56
common depth point 161, 165
common subexpression elimination 119
compiler 32, 38, 42, 75, 83, 107, 108, 114, 117–127, 132, 134, 240
complex instruction set computer (CISC) 26, 27, 29, 37
computed tomography 213
computer animation 5, 181
Computer Generated Imagery 218
concurrent 127, 131
Connection Machine (CM) 20, 71, 83, 85, 86, 92, 115, 134, 167, 172, 178, 186, 212, 239
constant folding 118, 120
constraints, optimization problem 198
Control Data Corporation 16, 65–66
control dependence 130
Convex Computer Corporation 85, 235
copy propagation 120
Cornell University 139, 231
Cosmic Cube 20
Cost/Performance 8, 25, 92
cost improvement 202
COUNT 111
COW 91
crack propagation 153
crash analysis 154

Index

Cray Research, Inc. 3, 16, 19, 20, 25, 37, 65, 70, 92, 103, 178, 235
    CRAY-1 20, 65, 66
    T3D 20, 37
    Y-MP 103
crew scheduling 198, 204, 205, 206, 212
crossbar switch 48, 70
CSHIFT 111
CYBER 16, 66
cyclic distribution 114

daemon 135, 240
DAP 172
Darwin 187
DASH 80, 91
database 5, 6, 138, 183–184
database query 184
data decomposition 152
data mining 6, 186–187
data parallelism 95, 115, 239
data partitioning 76
deadheading 204
DEALLOCATE (Fortran 90 statement) 109
DEC 20, 37, 92, 94, 235
decision support 184, 185, 187
DECODE 30
deconvolution 163
dendrite 174
Denelcor 19
dependence analysis 129, 132
derivatives 188, 190
diet problem 199
differential equations 10, 143, 151, 153
Digital Equipment Corp. (DEC) 20, 37, 92, 94, 235

directory-based cache coherence 79
discretization 149, 151, 240
disk array 14
Distributed Array Procesor (DAP) 172
distributed memory 75, 80–82, 85, 87, 113, 114, 137, 138, 195, 210, 240
DNA 169
Dobson, Mark 190
domain decomposition 144, 153
DOTPRODUCT (Fortran dot product) 64, 109
DRAM 33, 41–43
Droegmeier, Kelvin 156
dynamic programming 172

electrostatic force 173
embarrassingly parallel 212
Emory University 135
enzymes 170
EOSHIFT 111
Epsilon 184, 186
ethernet 48
Euler equations 146, 147
evolving processes 179
EXECUTE 30
expressions simplification 118

fat-tree network 53
fault tolerance 98, 136, 138, 240
FDDI 99
feasability 201, 203
FETCH 30
FIFO 219
financial applications 6, 10, 183
financial instrument pricing 183
finite differences 144, 148, 150–153, 155, 166, 240

finite element method 144, 151–155, 168, 241
Floating Point Systems 17
FLOPS 27–29, 32, 33
flow dependence 129–130
flow vector 201
fluid flow 145–147, 154
FORALL 112–113
Fortran 15, 38, 83, 108, 115, 124, 126, 191, 195, 241
Fortran-90 83, 108, 112, 116, 124, 125, 191
FPS 17

GATHER 16, 64, 117
Geco-Prakla 167
Gelernter, David 136
genetic algorithms 181, 187
geophone 160, 161
geophysics 160–161
GF-11 71
Gigawall 221
global local programming model 114
global programming model 82
Goodyear 70
grand challenge 4
Grant Tensor 167
graph 46
graphics 213
graphics pipeline 218–219

HDTV 213
heat conduction 144, 145, 149
HEP 19
Heterogeneous Element Processor 19
heterogeneous systems 136
Hewlett-Packard 92, 235
hidden image problem 216
high definition television 213
High Performance Fortran 15, 95, 112–114, 191
High Performance Fortran Forum 112
HiPPI 99, 241
homology modeling 172
HPF 15, 95, 112–114, 191
HPF ALIGN directive 113, 114
HPF DISTRIBUTE directive 114
HPF PROCESSORS directive 113
HPF TEMPLATE directive 114
Human Genome Project 169
hydrogen bonds 173
hydrophobic interactions 173
hypercube 20, 49–53

i860 20, 219
IBM 41, 71, 88, 178, 235
ILLIAC-IV 17, 68, 70–71
illumination models 214
in-arc 203
incompressible flow 146
Informix 185, 235
instruction scheduling 32
integer programming 206
Intel 20, 37, 83, 92, 103, 134, 167, 172, 178, 185, 212, 219, 235
intelligent business software 187
interest rate scenario 208, 209
interleaved memory 40
Internet 135
intrinsic functions 109, 111, 112, 116
  ALL 111
  ALLOCATED 111
  ANY 111
  COUNT 111

Index

CSHIFT 111
EOSHIFT 111
LBOUND 111
MAXLOC 111
MAXVAL 111
MERGE 111
MINLOC 111
MINVAL 111
PACK 111
PRODUCT 109
RESHAPE 111
SUM 109, 195
TRANSPOSE 111
UBOUND 111
UNPACK 111
I/O 86, 94, 97–103
iPSC 178
ISIS 138

Kendall Square Research 90, 103, 236

Lamport, Leslie 139
Laplace's equation 145
latency 28, 33, 36, 45, 94
lattice gas 180
Lawrence Livermore National Laboratory 228
LBOUND 111
least recently used (LRU) 39, 40, 241
Linda 136
linear network 48
linear programming 198, 200, 202, 206, 211
load balancing 76
logarithmic network 47
Los Alamos National Laboratory 86, 229

low velocity level 165
LRU 39, 40, 241

Mach 133
machine instructions 26–27
Macintosh 213
magnetic resource imaging 213
MasPar 71, 178, 236
Massachusetts Institute of Technology 80
MATMUL (Fortran matrix multiply) 64, 109
MAXLOC 111
MAXVAL 111
MBS 206, 208
MCF 201, 202
Meiko Scientific Computers 103, 228, 236
memory-based reasoning 177, 179
memory bottleneck 33, 36
memory hierarchy 13, 33, 35, 79–81
memory systems 13, 75
MERGE 111
mesh network 54, 68, 70
message passing 82, 83, 134–135, 241
Message Passing Initiative 137
message routing 48, 53, 57
microcode 26, 28, 29, 242
micromarketing 186
midpoint 161
migration 163, 166
MIMD 14, 18, 135, 156, 242
minimum cost flow 201, 202
MINLOC 111
MINVAL 111
MIPS 26–29, 32, 33, 80, 91, 219, 242

MISD 14, 242
MIT 80
Mobil 167
molecular biology 170, 181
Monte Carlo simulation 209
mortgage-backed securities 206, 208
MPI 137
MPP 45, 48, 70, 71, 85, 90–93, 132–135, 167, 174, 178, 184, 185, 241
MRI 213
multimedia 56
multiobjective optimization 207
multiple instruction issue 31–32, 34, 37, 41, 242
multiple instruction, multiple data (MIMD) 14, 18, 135, 156, 242
multiple instruction, single data (MISD) 14, 242
multiprocessor, multiple processor 13, 17, 18, 25, 37, 43, 45, 61, 73–90, 92–93, 107, 126, 132–137, 242
mutual exclusion 19, 137, 204, 242

NASA 68, 70
NASA Ames 230
NASA Langley 230
National Center for Atmospheric Research (NCAR) 231
National Center for Supercomputer Applications 222, 228, 231
National Energy Research Supercomputer Center 229
Navier–Stokes equations 147, 168, 180
NCAR 231
NCR 236

NCSA 222, 228, 231
NCSA Mosaic 228
nCUBE 103, 236
Newtonian fluid 147
network 45–58
network connectivity 45–46, 48–50, 54
network, logarithmic 47
network of workstations (NOW) 21, 44, 91–96
network topology 45, 48
neural network 174–175, 177, 179
neurode 175
NFS 97
NMO 163, 164, 165
non-uniform memory access (NUMA) 75, 81
normal distribution 190
normal moveout 163, 164, 165
NOW 21, 44, 91–96
NP-complete 202
NT 133
NUMA 75, 81
NUMBER_OF_PROCESSORS() 112, 193
numerical windtunnel 6, 144

Oak Ridge National Laboratory 135, 229
ocean models 156
oil industry 5, 10, 144, 159
Omega network 47–49
operating systems 132–135
optimization 6, 152, 197–212, 242
optimization, compiler 118–123
option 7, 188, 207
option adjusted spread 208, 210
Oracle 185, 236
Orca 133

Index

out-arc 203
output dependence 129

PACK 111
Paragon 20, 134
parallel I/O 98
parallelism 14, 61, 68, 73, 74, 82, 85, 126, 132, 218, 222, 242
parallelism in graphics 218
parallelism in virtual reality 222
parallelization 123, 126–127, 191, 242
parallel prefix operation 46
Parallel Virtual Machine 135, 139, 243
partial differential equations 143, 151, 153
pattern recognition 177
PDE 143, 151, 153
peak performance 7, 8, 25, 33, 71, 86, 243
perfect fluid 146
performance
    peak 7, 8, 25, 33, 71, 86, 243
    sustained 7, 8, 86
petroleum 160, 161, 162
pharmaceutical 6, 10, 170
pipeline, pipelining 13, 20, 28, 30–31, 34, 37, 41, 61, 62, 63, 65, 74, 123, 124, 129, 243
Pittsburgh Supercomputer Center 232
pixel 216
portfolio management 197, 206, 207, 211, 212
PowerPC 41
prefetch 36, 243
problem decomposition 152
processor shape 113

PRODUCT 109
programming languages 107, 124
programming model 82, 243
    global 82
    message passing 82–83
    thread 82
protein structure modeling 10, 169–170
PVM 135, 139, 243

QCD 5, 71
quaternary structure of protein 171
Quantum 186
quantum chromodynamics 5, 71

radar 161
RAID 14, 86, 97–98
rasterization 220
ratio test 203
ray tracing 213, 214, 216
realistic image synthesis 213, 214, 216
RealityEngine 219
reduced instruction set computer (RISC) 29–32, 36, 37, 41, 86, 123, 243
reduction functions 109
redundant array of inexpensive disks 14, 86, 97–98
remote procedure call 133
rendering 213
reservoir modeling 6, 10, 167–168, 214
RESHAPE 111
residual statics corrections 165
residue 170
Reynolds 147
ring network 48–49

RISC 29–32, 36, 37, 41, 86, 123, 243
risk-aversion 211
RNA 169
RPC 133
RS6000 178

Sandia National Laboratory 229
San Diego Supercomputer Center 232
scalability 79, 90, 92, 243
SCATTER 16, 64, 117
scheduling 32
Scholes, Myron 189
scoreboard 32, 243
secondary structure of protein 170
seismic processing 10, 159–168
semiconductor 5
sequence comparison 171
Sequent 185, 236
SGI (Silicon Graphics Incorporated) 80, 86, 91, 219, 223, 236
SHAPE 111
shared memory 19, 61, 75, 76, 79–81, 86, 90, 133, 136, 138, 243
Silicon Graphics Incorporated 80, 86, 91, 219, 223, 236
SIMD 14, 18, 19, 61, 66–68, 70–71, 87, 156, 244
Simplex method 198, 202, 203, 206, 211
single instruction, multiple data (SIMD) 14, 18, 19, 61, 66–68, 70–71, 87, 156, 244
single instruction, single data (SISD) 14, 244
single program, multiple data (SPMD) 84, 156, 244

SISD 14, 244
SIZE 111
SMP 84, 185, 244
snoopy-based cache coherence 79
software 107–140
software pipelining 129, 244
solution method 143, 148
soma 174
sound wave shot 161–162
SP1 88
spanning tree 203
SPARC 20, 86
speech recognition 177
speech synthesis 177
speedup 8, 79, 244
SPMD 84, 156, 244
spread 208
SRAM 33
SQL 185
stack 161, 163, 165
Stanford DASH 80, 91
Stanford University 80, 91
Star-100 65
stochastic processes 190, 195
STORE 30
Stratus Computer Inc. 139, 236
structural analysis 153
subproblem solution 205
SUM 109, 195
superscalar 29, 32, 36, 37, 41, 71, 123, 244
sustained performance 7, 8, 86
switch 46–48, 57, 244
Sybase 185, 237
symmetric multiprocessor 84, 185, 244
synapse 174
synchronization 19, 56, 75, 76, 83, 84, 127, 134, 135

Index

synchronous transfer mode 57
synoptic weight 175
systolic 61

T3D 20, 37
Tandem 185, 237
teraflop 4, 244
tertiary structure of protein 171
Texas Instruments 16, 64
texture mapping 219
Theory Center 231
Thinking Machines Corporation 20,
    71, 83, 85, 86, 92, 103, 115,
    134, 167, 172, 178, 186,
    187, 212, 237
thread 82, 84
TI 16, 64
toroidal network 54, 70
training, neural network 176
    graded 176
    self-supervised 176
    supervised 176
    unsupervised 176
transaction processing 185
TRANSPOSE 111
traveling salesman 198, 202
traveltime, of a wave 164
tuple space 136
turbulence 147, 154

UBOUND 111
University of Oklahoma 156
UNPACK 111
useless code elimination 122

valuation analysis 208, 209
Van der Waals force 173
vector 13, 15, 16, 61–70, 73, 74, 85,
    86, 124, 244, 245
vectorization 123–124, 244

velocity analysis 163, 164
very long instruction word 245
virtual circuit interface 57
virtual reality 5, 10, 213, 221
visualization 5, 214, 220, 221
VLIW 245
VLSI 20
volatility 209
voxel 216

weathering layer 165
Western Geophysical 167
WHERE 111
windtunnel 6, 144
write-invalidate 77
write-update 78

x-ray crystallography 172

Yale University 136